A Cosmic Cornucopia

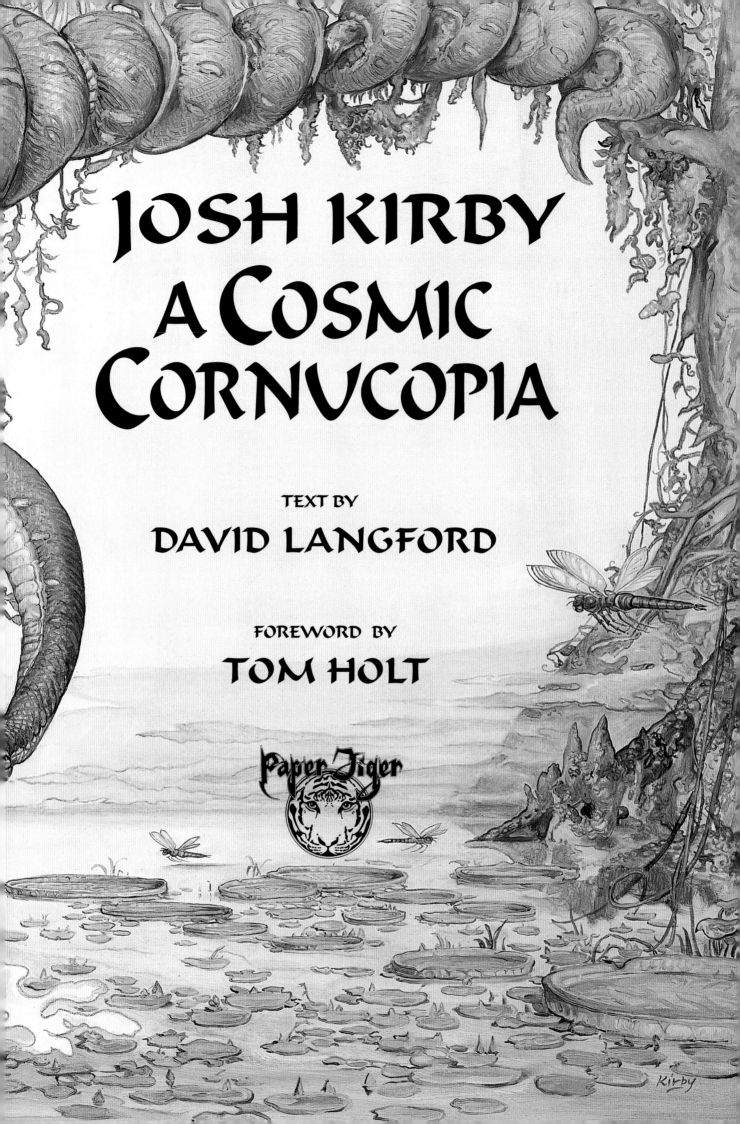

JOSH KIRBY
A COSMIC
CORNUCOPIA

TEXT BY

DAVID LANGFORD

FOREWORD BY

TOM HOLT

Paper Tiger

First published in Great Britain in 1999
by Paper Tiger
an imprint of Collins & Brown Limited
London House
Great Eastern Wharf
Parkgate Road
London SW11 4NQ
www.papertiger.co.uk

Distributed in the United States and Canada by Sterling Publishing Co,
387 Park Avenue South, New York, NY 10016, USA.

9 8 7 6 5 4 3 2 1

British Library Cataloguing-in-Publication Data:
A catalogue record for this book
is available from the British Library.

ISBN 1 85585 731 6

Commissioning editor: Paul Barnett
Designer: Malcolm Couch

Reproduction by Global Colour, Malaysia
Printed and bound in by Dai Nippon Printing Co. (HK) Ltd, Hong Kong

CONTENTS

FOREWORD

For the soldier, the Victoria Cross; for the scientist, the Nobel prize; for the journalist, the Pulitzer. For those of us who nibble at the cheese-face of comic fantasy, however, the ultimate decoration is that ubiquitous but unique artefact, the Kirby cover.

You see them everywhere. Walk the length of any train and they wink at you. They are resplendent on the shelves of Borders or W. H. Smith, like a lovingly tended flowerbed in a municipal garden. You catch fleeting glimpses of them, shoved halfway into the pockets of passers-by. In the houses of strangers, they grin at you from bookshelves and tabletops like old friends. They glow like mosaic tiles scattered across drab tarmac. Wherever two or three are gathered together with big, soppy grins on their faces, there is Kirby also.

The author's first glimpse of his or her first Kirby cover is an unforgettable experience. Mine was a glorious thing ('and bloody well wasted on you,' my wife pointed out): a dramatic swathe of blue sea and moonlight, combined with a perspective you shouldn't really be able to wedge into a mere two dimensions. When I saw it for the first time – it's the cover for *Flying Dutch* (see opposite) – I felt that someone had reached into my mind and pulled out the book, not as it had turned out but as I wished it had been. For the first time, I actually wanted to read the wretched thing.

For me, Josh Kirby's work is about space – the ability to combine panoramic satellite's-eye views with minute, bustling detail (and still leave room for the title and the information that this edition is not for sale in the USA; well, quite). His palette gleams with colours that you simply can't buy in the shops; if anybody could mix up a brushful of octarine, he could. He understands light and, perhaps more importantly, he understands shadows; he knows how light gets grubby and shop-soiled when it has to crawl in under the sweaty armpits of the customers in a dingy tavern, or how it slowly dies in a prison. As for his people and animals and . . . well, things (which are invariably things of beauty and joys forever), they're straight out of the hall of mirrors: close enough to reality to be immediately familiar, but thinned down, puffed out, spindled, folded, and translated (in the mathematical sense) into a fourth dimension of comedy. Kirby is a cartoonist in oils; his understanding of and sympathy for the characters he creates is obvious in every wicked grin and horrified rictus. Above all, he's capable of grandeur. And he can do curtains.

I asked someone who knows about such things who he thought Kirby's main influences might be. From Titian and Rubens, he said, a delight in form and (no other word for it) bulk. From Hogarth, the ability to characterize, to convey information. From Bosch, an overflowing, visceral imagination. And from Bruegel the abundance of bustling, imperfect humanity. These are impressive references to find in the work of an extremely professional and successful commercial artist, of whose work there are literally millions of copies in circulation. Perhaps that's one of the reasons why Kirby succeeds so well in a notoriously difficult genre – there's never a sense of dumbing down, of sacrificing vision or ambition to Unspeakable Commerce.

Maybe that's an advantage of working in comedy; and Kirby is, quite simply, the funniest artist living. I have a feeling that, if he were

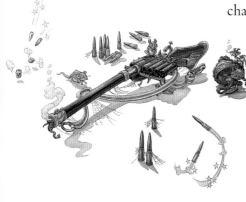

Detail from back cover for *Men at Arms* by Terry Pratchett (Gollancz 1993), showing the newly invented 'gonne' which inspires a serial killer. The swamp dragon and helmet were transferred to the book's spine, and Gollancz deleted the bullets at front and left. Their cartoon-like motion lines intentionally suggest a sketch made by the gun's inventor Leonard of Quirm.

The remoteness of the Flying Dutchman's and his immortal crew's exile is graphically evoked in this cover for *Flying Dutch* (Orbit 1991) by Tom Holt. Kirby's eye for manic detail even takes in the crazed sailor van Doorning who hopes one day to achieve suicide – despite alchemically induced invulnerability – by repeatedly diving from the top of the mainmast.

to draw you a sketch-map showing you how to get to the bus station, it'd be hilarious. Comedy isn't something you can synthesize; you can't ersatz it out of soya beans, and you can't make it if it isn't already there. It's an approach to life, a way of seeing things. Kirby has the comic filter over his lens at all times.

It is of course through his collaboration with Terry Pratchett that Josh Kirby is today best known. This begs an unanswerable question – how important has his contribution been to the Pratchett phenomenon? A book jacket serves several purposes, apart from its primary function of keeping the coffee and the tarka dal off the rest. It has to tell you, subliminally, what sort of book this is, what other books it's like, whether it's the sort of thing you're likely to enjoy – all this in a sixtieth of a second at twenty-five paces across a crowded Waterstones. Arguably, Josh Kirby is too skilful at these things for his own good: every clonemaster and purveyor of Pratchett Lite wants either a Kirby or the Kirby look; the Look is diluted by the efforts of imitators; familiarity breeds what it breeds best, and the real thing suffers in our estimation as a result. Arguably, that goes with the territory for all creators of cultural icons; we begin to see what we expect to see, not what's actually there. It's a fact of life that someone as successful as Kirby, someone so immediately identified with one product, one genre, should find himself being restricted by his own success, required to do The Same, Only Different, over and over again for ever (which, for a creative artist, must be as good a definition of Hell as you're likely to get).

Because Kirby is so individualistic, so inimitable (a statement that's been conclusively proved by exhaustive experimental research on the part of the publishing industry), my guess is that his work will survive, and in time come to be seen separately from its colossal associate. I'm not sure what it is exactly, but there's something about Kirby that reminds me of Arthur Rackham, another illustrator whose work has managed to detach itself and stand alone. It'll depend, I guess, on posterity's attitudes to comedy and success (both of which seem to be fatal obstacles to respectability in our time). Contrary to received opinion, though, it's not actually obligatory for someone to be dead before his work can be discovered to be really rather good.

Enjoy.

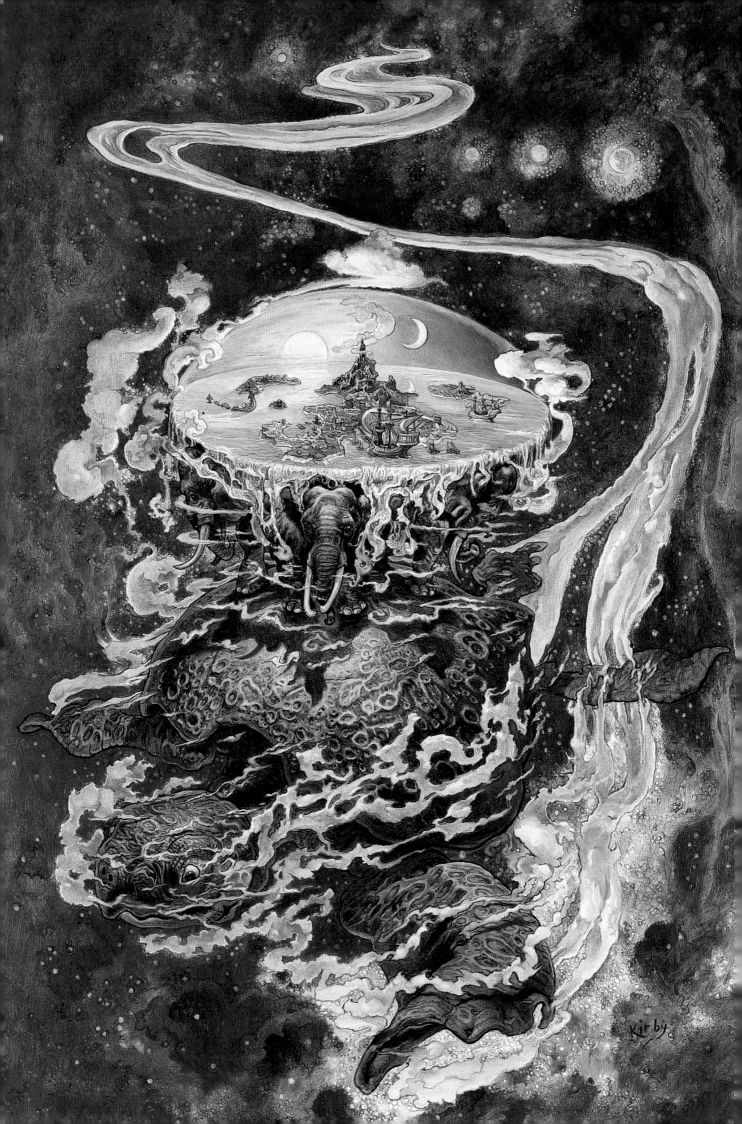

Biographical Introduction

Josh Kirby was born a long time ago and refers to himself as 'unbearably ancient' . . . Terry Pratchett, who knows a thing or two, has darkly hinted at an age of several centuries.[1] At birth he was christened Ronald William Kirby; the 'Josh' was to come later. He remembers that even as a small boy he had a particular career in mind: 'At seven years old I drew a "trade sign" – ARTIST – for my future life.'

In due course he studied art techniques for six years at the Liverpool City School of Art (1943–9), where his drawing course brought him the Intermediate certificate in Arts and Crafts and was followed by a painting course that led to his National Diploma in Design. It was here at the school that he picked up the nickname which became his working name: 'When I was at Art School, some wag thought I painted like Sir Joshua Reynolds!'

Today Kirby doesn't feel that his mature style owes anything in particular to the tuition he received in Liverpool. When asked about influences, he most often names three past artists. The oldest is Hieronymus Bosch (?1450–1516), famous for those teeming, surreally fantastic landscapes of heaven and hell – including the Garden of Earthly Delights whose name was echoed in the Kirby collection *In the Garden of Unearthly Delights*. Next comes Pieter Bruegel the Elder (?1525–1569) with his hauntingly detailed groups of warts-and-all Flemish peasants, not to mention the definitive portrayal of the colossal Tower of Babel which Kirby later spoofed in his movie poster for *Monty Python's Life of Brian*. Least familiar to ordinary readers, there's the muralist Frank Brangwyn (1867–1956), who made bold use of colour and monumental compositions on a large scale. Of all three our artist says, 'I try to become more like these whilst contributing my personal viewpoint.'

What does he most value about his artistic heroes? 'The inventiveness of their imagery and the beauty of their techniques, especially that of Bruegel, whose close observation of nature adds an extra dimension of humanity to the teeming fantastic imagery of the paintings.'

After an early commission by Liverpool City Council to paint their Mayor – quite an honour for an artist at the beginning of his career – Kirby decided against the staid life of portrait-painting which had seemed a possibility while in art school. Instead he headed south for London to work for Pulford Publicity, a studio that produced film posters. This continued for years, varied by an interlude of poster work for a movie company in Paris. All along, though, he wanted a freelance career.

According to his own records his first published cover painting was produced in 1954 for *Cee-Tee Man*, a now largely forgotten 1955 science fiction novel by Dan Morgan. He touched the edge of the blockbuster James Bond phenomenon with a cover for the first Pan paperback edition of Ian Fleming's *Moonraker*, in 1956. But, as he happily admits, the realization that he truly wanted to make illustration his life's work came

Facing page:
Discworld II. One of Kirby's several lovingly detailed paintings of Terry Pratchett's Discworld as a whole – spinning atop four elephants who stand on the turtle Great A'Tuin as he, or just possibly she, swims forever through space. This appeared as the cover of *The Josh Kirby Discworld Portfolio* (Paper Tiger 1993, with text by Nigel Suckling).

---

[1] So the date 27 November 1928 can have no possible relevance.

This *Terry Pratchett Portrait* (1993, not previously published) applies Kirby's favourite 'Arcimboldo' or *Illustrated Man* facial technique – see Things That Go Bump – to the Pratchett features. Death swings a scythe around the edges of this face and Rincewind lurks between the eyes.

with a series of SF covers and interiors for *Authentic SF* magazine in 1956–7. This pointed the way to what Kirby most enjoyed doing.

A little-known fact about his work for *Authentic* is that much of it was signed 'Adash' or 'A-' . . . an intentional nod to the Non-Aristotelian or Null-A (Ā) multi-valued logic recommended in Count Alfred Korzybski's 1930s philosophy of 'General Semantics'. This had been quite influential in the SF world after being popularized, not altogether comprehensibly, by A.E. van Vogt in his 1948 cult novel *The World of Null-A*.

Since then, Kirby's work has appeared on the books of numerous SF, fantasy and horror authors – indeed, very many more than fans who identify him with Terry Pratchett's Discworld may realize. His personal list of published book covers from 1954 to 1999 runs to over 400 items, and is far from complete. For one thing, it deliberately excludes paintings which were done to order and required him to suppress his own distinctive style for, as he puts it, 'categories like War, Cowboy, Adventure, Romance . . . they don't hold any delights for me. And were done under sufferance so I could live and paint on a daily basis in a society that didn't care whether "artists" survived or not.'

Kirby's preferred medium is oil paint applied in thin layers, because this dries slowly, yet not too slowly, and can be easily retouched or overpainted – repeatedly, if need be. Over the years he has experimented with but eventually rejected various other art media, including watercolour, acrylic paint (which dries far too fast for his taste), gouache and even coloured pencils. After, in his own words, '*many* false starts' he produces a pencil rough of the chosen image, to be approved by the publisher's art editor . . . or, in the special case of Discworld, discussed over the phone with Terry Pratchett. Although it seems like simple common sense, this artist/author contact and feedback is unusual in the publishing world, where illustrators normally deal only with art editors. (Is it mere coincidence that authors are so frequently unhappy with their covers? Perish the thought.)

In earlier years Kirby often worked at very small scale, sometimes producing paintings hardly bigger than a paperback cover. As time went by his canvases tended to become larger, and he would expand his small pencil roughs to final size by the 'squaring-up' method that goes back to antiquity: dividing the sketch into small squares and using careful hand-eye coordination to copy the lines from each square to a corresponding grid of larger squares on the actual canvas (or, more often, size-coated watercolour board). Nowadays, a rare concession to technology, he makes use of a projector to ease the enlargement process. A Kirby oil painting takes its final shape at approximately four times the width and height of a wraparound paperback cover – front, spine and back – or about 18 ³/₄ in by 27 in (48 cm x 69 cm). If he is producing a front cover only, his usual size is 18 ³/₈ in by 11 ¹/₂ in (47 cm x 29 cm).

A slow worker, he reckons that it currently takes him four weeks to complete a single illustration, or eight counting the preliminary time taken to read a novel, select and visualize suitable images, and work out how they can be best presented. To the frustration of various authors who seriously covet them, he now prefers to keep all his original paintings . . . although in past times a few have been acquired by SF figures like Ray Bradbury and Forrest J. Ackerman – not to mention the Duke of Bedford.

With Discworld he found the perfect complement for the more fantastically humorous side of his talent. Cover paintings for Terry Pratchett's *The Colour of Magic* in 1983 and *The Light Fantastic* in 1986 quickly established Kirby as *the* illustrator for Discworld – inseparable, like Tenniel for Alice or E.H. Shepard for Winnie-the-Pooh. The Discworld connection has continued ever since, and earned him long-deserved international recognition as an artist.

It should be noted, though, that the cognoscenti appreciated Kirby long before fame dug him in the ribs. He has exhibited his paintings in London's Portal Gallery and ICA, in Berlin, and in many provincial British galleries. Visitors who went to the huge art show at the 1979 World SF Convention in Brighton voted him Best SF Artist (professional class) when Discworld was still years away.

Past collections of his work are: *The Voyage of the Ayeguy* (1981), a portfolio of six linked science-fantasy pictures rather than a book; *The Josh Kirby Poster Book* (1989), containing 13 posters inspired by Discworld; *In the Garden of Unearthly Delights* (1991), a large selection of 159 paintings; and *The Josh Kirby Discworld Portfolio* (1993), actually a book of 28 paintings rather than a portfolio. Large-format editions of *Eric* (1990), whose text is by Terry Pratchett, contain enough elaborate Kirby illustrations (15 plus cover) to qualify as another mini-collection – the artist receives equal front-cover credit.

A private Kirby ambition in recent years has been to find a building in London suitable for a permanent exhibition of his Discworld paintings. He'd like it 'to be called "Unseen University Museum Library and Art Gallery", and to house books and memorabilia in display cases as well as paintings hanging on the walls.' Despite hopes of using first a baroque orangery built in 1717 and then a Victorian bell tower, this project keeps being delayed by lack of funds and problems with access regulations: bell towers, for example, are not designed for wheelchairs. At present the gallery plan has officially 'gone into the doldrums'. One day, perhaps . . .

Meanwhile he lives and paints in an oversized Tudor rectory near Diss, Norfolk, which has space for multiple studios – a large room for large paintings and, logically enough, a small room for small ones. He cheerfully tells interviewers that he's a pauper, since the only way to get rich doing book covers is to work quickly, and: 'I work very, very slowly.' But it adds up to surprisingly many notable paintings over 45 years.

Terry Pratchett Portrait II (*Weekend Guardian* cover, 23 October 1993) – a more cheerful 'tattooed Pratchett' with a forehead full of favourite Discworld characters and the orang-utan Librarian brooding in the bosky recesses of his beard. Kirby offered the *Weekend Guardian* either of his two similar portraits, and they made the 'obvious' choice of this smiling version rather than the more sombre alternative.

Kirby rings the changes again in *Terry Pratchett Caricature* (*Weekend Guardian* 23 October 1993): the portraits impose Discworld imagery on essentially realistic Pratchett faces, but this one throws a less photographic version of him into Discworld – in fact, into the middle of Kirby's best-loved 'action tableau', with Rincewind and others clinging to the berserk Luggage.

CHAPTER ONE

DISCWORLD DELIGHTS

The original four-eyed Twoflower as seen on the cover of *The Colour of Magic*.

Inevitably, Josh Kirby is most widely known in Britain today for the exuberant cover paintings he produces for Terry Pratchett's phenomenally bestselling 'Discworld' novels. He himself feels that Discworld has inspired one of his two most personally satisfying and artistically successful series of book illustrations – the second being his covers for Robert Silverberg's 'Majipoor' science fantasies. And no other commercial paintings give Kirby so much sheer enjoyment and fun in creation as those of Discworld.

The faithfulness of Kirby's images to the text is frequently debated by the more enthusiastic Pratchett fans. Only with his first Pratchett commission, *The Colour of Magic*, does the cover art restrict itself to something like realism, with Twoflower the 'Auriental' tourist and Rincewind the failed wizard manically pursuing the former's self-propelled, psychopathic Luggage (with lots of lovingly rendered little legs) into that notorious low pub the Broken Drum. Even here, however, Kirby allows himself considerable artistic licence.

Perhaps the oddest aspect of that painting, a quirk repeated on the cover of Pratchett's follow-up book *The Light Fantastic*, is that Twoflower is disconcertingly shown with four eyes in one horizontal row. (Not quite as alarming as Alan Moore's comic-strip creation Abelard Snazz, The Man With The Two-Storey Brain, whose appearance was stolen from a book of optical illusions: Snazz's two pairs of eyes, one set above the other, are jarringly difficult to look at.) There is indeed support for four eyes in the text, where the first character to meet Twoflower 'found himself looking up into a face with four eyes in it'. Pratchett goes so far as to call Twoflower 'the four-eyed man'.

Of course the general consensus is that Pratchett was alluding – a little clumsily in those early days of Discworld – to the schoolboy epithet 'four-eyes' that was once applied to absolutely anyone with spectacles. So Twoflower, more or less the archetypal Japanese tourist, is simply wearing the glasses which are part of that cultural cliché. According to the vast Annotated Pratchett File that can be found on the Internet, Kirby's highly literal visualization of that phrase is regarded by his devotees as 'interpretative genius' and by non-fans as failure to get the joke.

Controversy may rage in the acrimonious forum of cyberspace, but Kirby himself is cheerfully frank: 'I didn't know it was meant as a joke! I was used to fantasy and accepted the statement as so.' He was not alone: the cover artist for the Estonian edition of *The Colour of Magic* made the identical error. In later Kirby paintings Twoflower has specs and a more plausible number of eyes.

As early as his second Discworld painting, Kirby established the exuberant 'action tableau' cover composition which recurs throughout the series of covers and is also echoed in non-Discworld cover paintings done in the same lush style. This approach takes a central image roughly representative of some scene or sequence from the novel, and surrounds it with further characters, props and fragments of background that take Kirby's fancy, lifted from anywhere in the text. The emphasis is on effective composition rather than slavish realism. As he says, 'I like to bring small scenes together if I can't find a single incident that represents the whole book.'

Early Discworld covers appeared in this book's companion collection *In the Garden of Unearthly Delights* and in *The Josh Kirby Discworld Portfolio*. The story continues several volumes further along in the sequence. . .

One of Pratchett's most improbably popular characters is Death, the skeletal Grim Reaper who always speaks IN HOLLOW, DOOMY CAPITALS, LIKE THIS. This terrifying entity does his Duty of taking life as he finds it, but is also obscurely on humanity's side – an eternal straight man whose poor grasp of human emotion generates much comic pathos. Pratchett softens the idea of the skull-face by specifying sparks of blue light in Death's eye-sockets, a lead which Kirby follows throughout.

In *Reaper Man*, where Death is made redundant and left with time on his hands, twin plot lines offer two cover opportunities. Instead of painting the high jinks in Ankh-Morpork city as the excitable wizards of Unseen

The Colour of Magic (1983) and *The Light Fantastic* (1986), 1999 omnibus edition from Colin Smythe Ltd, also used in the Ink Group's 1999 Discworld wall calendar. The painting combines elements from both books. In the foreground is the Discworld's Rim, where the sea pours forever over as the Rimfall; the central ship carries Rincewind, Death and – here, with hindsight, shown with his rightful glasses – the garishly clad tourist Twoflower.

Overleaf:
Reaper Man (Gollancz 1991) . . . the most gentle and pastoral of all the Discworld covers, this would look faintly menacing to a new reader who doesn't know that Discworld's Death is a softy at heart. Lurking in the middle distance is the prototype combine harvester which Death challenges to a scything match.

Whizzing Wizards – a first attempt, not actually used, at the cover painting for Terry Pratchett's *Moving Pictures* (1990), in which movie fever enters Discworld through a magical portal in the place called Holy Wood. This being Discworld, the cameras contain demons painting each frame of film *very fast*.

University cope with a plague of poltergeists and undead (triggered by the fact that Death is no longer collecting souls), Kirby produced a tranquil farm scene from the alternate narrative in which Death takes a job as an ungrim reaper in the cornfields. Hourglasses in the tree above are a reminder that time is still ticking away, for the temporarily mortal Death as well as humanity. *Reaper Man* introduced another popular figure, the Death of Rats or Grim Squeaker, here seen sitting on his master's knee. One of many animal-specific substitute Deaths that spontaneously come into being on Death's retirement, he's the only one to hold firmly on to an independent existence. Well, almost the only one: the Death of Rats is infested with the Death of Fleas. . .

Kirby has various little tricks for coping with the slowness of his painting methods, and one of them is to go ahead with a picture while the rough sketch is still being approved by an art editor or Terry Pratchett. This ploy to buy time can backfire when – horror of horrors – the rough isn't approved after all. So once in a while there's an extra, unused version of a Kirby cover.

This happened with Pratchett's *Moving Pictures*, whose unpublished rendition appears here. Comparing this with the book cover, we can see that the conflict was between Kirby's love of focusing the picture on an 'action tableau' – that hurtling wheelchair loaded with wizards – and Pratchett's sense that the movie-shooting elements should be brought more plausibly together. So for the final version, lusciously sprawling actress 'Delores de Syn' and accompanying figures are shifted to the right, close to the camera at far right, and the wizards are deported to the left. Thus, when this

painting became a wraparound cover, the love interest and the cameras were both on the front, and the wizards on the back.

One item that vanished altogether in the shuffle was Kirby's visualization of this movie-obsessed book's daftest image: a giant woman climbing Discworld's closest approximation to a skyscraper while clutching a terrified ape (the famous orang-utan Librarian of Unseen University). Shame!

Kirby's repeated use of the 'action tableau' echoes a provocative statement made in the 1997 *Encyclopedia of Fantasy* edited by John Clute and John Grant: that fantasy art is essentially a narrative form, that its imagery is dominated by the sense of *what happens next*. (The appearance of motion itself isn't necessary: for example, the semi-idyllic *Reaper Man* cover throbs with anticipatory suspense about what may follow – like the enigmatic pastoral snapshot-scene of Holman Hunt's *The Hireling Shepherd*.) That wheelchair-load of wizards, seemingly bound to crash into something before long, is careering from left to right. This adds to the effect of speed since, as every artist knows, the human eye is accustomed, at least in the West, to scan printed pages and images in this direction. Movement from right to left often seems more laboured, as though going 'against the grain'. But see the later *Hogfather* cover. . .

Lords and Ladies (1992) – the 1993 Corgi paperback cover, preferred by Kirby after a bad time with requested revisions to the hardback version. The Horned King is outsized in more ways than are visible, as hinted by Pratchett's mention that the entrance to this underground cavern bears a runic inscription translating as: 'I've Got A Great Big Tonker.'

There were likewise two covers for *Lords and Ladies*, the Discworld novel that sees the top witch Granny Weatherwax's tiny homeland of Lancre invaded by a horde of viciously sadistic elves. Kirby took against his first version, the wraparound jacket for Gollancz's, since 'the hardback experience was so traumatic for me.' It was already a difficult composition with many elements – elves with their Queen and Horned King, a unicorn, two of the witches, a ring of standing stones, the Librarian, bees and more – and Gollancz then decided that Kirby's cavern setting should be laboriously changed to an outdoor scene. Not to mention 'changing dead warriors arising out of their tombs into Morris men'. For the paperback Kirby simply redid the cover from scratch 'to suit *me*'.

The resulting image is simpler and stronger, showing the underground confrontation between aged reprobate witch Nanny Ogg (accompanied by Casanunda the bewigged dwarf Lothario) and a far more effectively massive Horned King. All the previous clutter has been stripped away, apart for a few token bees. The newly introduced snakes remind us in a wickedly obvious way that the King is also a symbol of potent, outsized masculinity. But, as Freud failed to remark, sometimes a snake is just a snake.

That certain slight friction between Kirby and the Gollancz design people had begun rather earlier. He likes the uniform layout which Corgi's paperbacks have kept to this day, with title and author in a neat rectangular panel. Gollancz dropped the panel in favour of bigger and bigger title/author lettering . . . in the artist's view, 'reducing the effectiveness of the painting and the overall distinctive look in relation to other hardbacks in the bookshops'.

With *Men at Arms* it seemed almost as though Gollancz wanted this *not* to look like a Terry Pratchett book. Huge lettering dominated a new white background which offered room for only a small 'detail' illustration rather than a full cover. 'It seemed to me that they (Gollancz) were indicating to me I should go away.' Nevertheless Kirby tackled the job with professional skill. The front cover shows the men and others of the Ankh-Morpork City Guard (Night Watch) in full charge: Cuddy the dwarf, Detritus the slow-witted troll, Angua the delectable werewolf, Carrot the fearless believer in actual justice, Nobby the almost human, and corpulent coward Sergeant Colon.

For the Corgi paperback's wraparound jacket, it was possible to add the lurking, gun-toting villain and give the charging group a background – an unobtrusive and restrained background, though, since the figures had been designed to stand alone and distracting features behind them would surely have mucked up the composition. Kirby: 'Oh, the agony!'

The new white background continued for a couple more books, to the despair of the artist: 'I felt I could no longer express myself. I tried to remember I could add a background for the Corgi edition, but this involved unnatural artistic contortions which made me physically ill. It is no way to design a painting!' When it came to *Interesting Times*, Kirby found it impossible to extract a suitable detail from his rough sketch

Men at Arms (Gollancz 1993) – a new look for the hardback. Kirby: 'Gollancz did not realize they were diluting the by now well known "livery" so identification started to depend on reading the lettering rather than the general look of the book – previously quite clear even across a bookshop.' (See also page 6.)

for a complete painting, and so was forced to paint separate pictures for hardback and paperback.

Interesting Times is Terry Pratchett's exercise in chinoiserie, cramming in everything we vaguely think we know about ancient and modern China. (It's the *1066 and All That* approach: history is defined as the bits we remember.) In the cover we see the inept wizard Rincewind, Kirby's favourite Discworld character – 'I like his determined and dedicated cowardice!' – who has just been magically transported from Unseen University to the pseudo-Chinese 'Agatean Empire'. Naturally there is a Great Wall. The 'four-eyed' character Twoflower, a native of these parts, reappears at the left with the originally intended spectacles.

Reading the book reveals that the peculiar airborne metal object in front of Rincewind is a Barking Dog, an ornately designed black-powder cannon (the Agateans are *good* at pyrotechnics) which is in process of being teleported to Unseen University far across the Discworld in order to balance the arriving mass of Rincewind. This, as Pratchett would say, is because of quantum.

The agonies of *Interesting Times* led to a crisis point. 'I decided to give up doing Terry Pratchett covers . . . but a compromise was reached, i.e. showing the whole wraparound painting on the front cover – a view through a letterbox, as it were.'

The first Discworld book to receive the letterbox treatment was *Maskerade*, entangling witches Granny Weatherwax and Nanny Ogg in a twisted replay of *The Phantom of the Opera*. Its Ankh-Morpork Opera

Interesting Times II – after reluctantly providing mere 'detail' art to go on a white background for the 1994 hardback first edition, Kirby was able to spread himself with this 1995 Corgi paperback cover. The chained figure in the foreground is the nonagenarian warrior Cohen the Barbarian – 'a lifetime in his own legend'.

Overleaf:
Men at Arms II (Corgi paperback 1994) . . . the picture is extended to show the dread gunman of Ankh-Morpork standing on an annoyed-looking gargoyle as he takes aim. The 'gonne' described in the book is clearly a rifle; here Kirby increases its visibility by making it a kind of blunderbuss.

Maskerade (Gollancz 1995). This crowded cover, painted as a wraparound, was reduced to a narrow 'letter-box' slot on the front of the hardback. The back cover carried the same shrunken image, but mirror-reversed – a common publishers' practice which Kirby particularly dislikes.

Facing page, top:
Feet of Clay (Gollancz 1996). Here Kirby cheekily incorporates and emphasizes Pratchett's clues to the identity of a poisoner and the means by which arsenic is administered to the wary, closely guarded victim. The coat of arms is based on one of several sketches drawn by Stephen Briggs for the book's interior.

Facing page, below:
Hogfather by Terry Pratchett (Gollancz 1996): an overt celebration of that favourite spiral composition which one fan has dubbed the Kirby Kurl Konstant – see Magic (Un)Realism. Part of this design was used on 'Merry Hogswatch!' greetings cards given away with the Christmas 1997 issue of *SFX* magazine.

House setting inspired Kirby to go to town on the expensive, ormolu-encrusted interior, with a dizzying aerial perspective that takes in the upper circle – where Nanny Ogg is getting over-excited while her appalling cat Greebo clings to her hat – the stalls, the stage where the traditional over-weight tenor and soprano are giving their all, and even the orchestra pit. Right at the back of the stage, the masked Phantom lurks. . .

Pratchett returned to the Ankh-Morpork Watch and his special subgenre of Discworld police-procedural fantasy in *Feet of Clay*. This title refers to the golems employed as slave labour in the city. The Jewish golem legend, in its most famous form, tells of the 16th-century Rabbi Lowe's animation of a clay man to defend the Prague ghetto against an imperial pogrom. Discworld golems are clay statues powered by magic words, regarded as tireless robots programmed only to work and obey . . . but they're secretly discontented with getting all the filthiest jobs, and try to manufacture their own leader and defender. This plan not only goes awry but also intersects a devious plot to poison the city's efficient though unloved ruler, the Patrician, with arsenic. Samuel Vimes of the Watch is confronted with a genuine puzzle in detection, while a rogue golem stalks the streets by night.

Kirby's visualization of the unstoppable golem figure is partly based on recollection of the classic German movie *The Golem* (1920), which retells Rabbi Lowe's story. Additionally, 'Terry sent me a little "scribble" as a guide.' Pratchett also specified the glowing red eyes in his book.

In *Hogfather*, the title character is Discworld's Father Christmas – currently put out of action by an assassin hired by the sinister Auditors of Reality, who hate emotion, myth, fantasy and anything that makes the world seem tolerable. With many a hollow-voiced HO HO HO, Death takes

Another rueful Kirby confession: this unpublished painting for *Jingo* (1997) was 'the victim of my "jumping the gun" as I was convinced that the first rough was the *very* way to do it. Gollancz disagreed, with no explanation other than "it gave away the plot".' The low-tech breathing and motive arrangements of Discworld's first submarine are meticulously imagined – very much in the spirit of W. Heath Robinson.

Jingo II (Gollancz 1997) . . . a picture showing particular attention to detail, if not to time-sequence. The weathercock that's the first sign of a sunken island rising from the deeps is carefully lettered for the unique compass-points of Discworld: Hubward, Rimward, Turnwise and Widdershins.

over the Hogfather's work of delivering Hogswatchnight presents, and is here seen driving the legendary sleigh that's hauled through the skies by mighty porkers Gouger, Snouter, Tusker and Rooter. The assassin Mr Teatime is visible at lower right, and characters from various parts of the story cling to the sleigh, including Death's adoptive granddaughter Susan (with scythe). The right-to-left flight of the great pigs suggests not excessive speed but some difficulty of progress: air resistance, of course, as despite a certain lack of aerodynamic shape they laboriously soar.

As with *Moving Pictures*, there are two *Jingo* pictures because Kirby was pleased enough with his first rough to assume that it *had* to be approved, and incautiously started painting. Pratchett's plot deals with the threat of

war between the city-state of Ankh-Morpork and the land of Klatch (the Arabia of Discworld), triggered when the sunken island of Leshp rises in the Circle Sea which separates them and is claimed by both. Since the bone-domed artist/inventor Leonard of Quirm has fortuitously devised a primitive submarine, the Patrician of Ankh-Morpork conscripts him and the two most useless Watchmen (Nobby and Colon) for the secret under-sea mission that inspired this splendidly claustrophic interior. This was the first time that Kirby had painted Leonard, who looks just as expected; the Patrician's usual black outfit has become red to prevent him from fading into the shadows. Alas, it was decided in high places that the submarine's existence – not revealed until halfway through *Jingo* – shouldn't be given away by the cover.

Vampires and witches – the latter represented by Nanny Ogg and young Magrat – are easily identified in this painting for *Carpe Jugulum* (Doubleday 1998). The teeming little blue men are a clan of light-fingered gnomes with terrible Scots accents . . . that is, pictsies.

In the picture that was in fact used, Kirby plays his frequent trick of mixing elements from various parts of the timeline, including the first sign of Leshp's surfacing – the weathercock, already being disputed by citizens of both nations. At the left is the Klatchian ship on which, later in the story, luscious werewolf Angua of the Ankh-Morpork Watch is held captive; at right is the pursuing vessel commandeered by Vimes and the Watch. The magic carpet carries the Patrician and the rest of the submarine's contingent: in the text, Leonard is in fact left minding the boat while the other three explore Klatch, but after working out his appearance Kirby was clearly determined to keep Leonard in the painting. Even the tiniest of bit-part players, the briefly mentioned Curious Squid, has its place.

The Gollancz letterbox-format compromise had continued from *Maskerade* through *Hogfather*, *Feet of Clay* and *Jingo*. Then came an

The Last Continent
(Doubleday 1998) . . . this
evocation of the strangely
Australia-like Discworld
continent known as XXXX
or Terror Incognita features
Rincewind (the cowards'
coward) perpetually on the
run as usual, but this time
with corks dangling round
his pointy hat.

upheaval in Discworld traditions, as Terry Pratchett switched hardback publishers – moving from Gollancz to Transworld's Doubleday imprint and bringing hardcover and paperback editions under the same roof, since Transworld also produce Corgi paperbacks. Looking backward over decades of interaction with publishers, Kirby had already remarked: 'I feel most comfortable with Corgi Books.' And sure enough, his artwork was given more space on Pratchett's first Transworld/Doubleday hardbacks, *The Last Continent* and *Carpe Jugulum*.

The Last Continent is a madcap progress through a land which in Pratchett's words is not Australia but 'somewhere entirely different which just happens to be, here and there, a bit . . . Australian'. Its slightly shambolic plot is in part a vehicle for introducing every possible Aussie joke or reference that came to mind. Kirby was able to pick and choose for another manic 'action tableau' of Rincewind clinging to a speeding kangaroo while being pursued through a desert full of skulls and lager cans by deadly spiders and snakes, a low-tech *Mad Max* cavalcade, and a Luggage whose footgear has been strangely influenced by the local tradition of drag acts. Ayers Rock inevitably looms on the horizon.

(The wizards in the background, behind and beneath a window which is a space/time portal from Unseen University, have been hauled in from another plotline taking place on an entirely different island. Such, again, is the awesome power of Artistic Licence.)

Next came *Carpe Jugulum* – Discworld dog-Latin for 'Go for the throat' – in which Pratchett confronts his seemingly undefeatable witch Granny Weatherwax with her most serious challenge. Granny's power and laser-willed belief in herself have so far dealt with all opposition, including wizards, an entire tribe of nasty elves and her own evil sister. This time, though, the menace to Lancre is a family of new-breed vampires who through long training are immune to garlic, sunlight, crosses, holy water and all the rest of the vampire-hunter's paraphernalia, and who are

Cover for Pratchett's *The Fifth Elephant* (Doubleday 1999), echoing the movie title *The Fifth Element*. Discworld notoriously rests on four gigantic elephants. Legend tells of a fifth that fell off the turtle into a decaying orbit and crashed to earth in a fiery 'asteroid impact', laying down the vast underground fat deposits still mined by the dwarfs of Uberwald.

physically, mentally and magically far tougher than Granny. Excessive deviousness is called for.

The magpies in this picture are used telepathically as long-range spies by the vampiric Count Magpyr of Uberwald – a Pratchettian place-name which is German for 'over the wood', suggesting Transylvania, 'across the woods'.

Uberwald, centre of Discworld spookiness and undead activism, is likewise the setting for *The Fifth Elephant*. Vimes, his wife Lady Sybil and selected members of the Watch travel there on what is ostensibly a diplomatic mission on behalf of Ankh-Morpork but in fact develops complications on three fronts. The dwarfs are in a tizzy because the Scone of Stone on which their new king must be crowned has been stolen – a classic impossible crime in a locked room. A local vampire is sinisterly manipulative. And the werewolves, even more implacable and unkillable than vampires, set up Vimes to be their defenceless quarry in a long, gruelling hunt. Things get very tense indeed.

One slightly awkward aspect of Kirby's deep involvement with Discworld is that people tend to assume he must be raking in pots of money from his association with this amazing string of bestsellers. Unfortunately, the publishing industry is traditionally tough on cover artists. Authors get more royalties for every book sold; artists get a one-off fee. As a result, Kirby has become a rueful victim of his own success.

The snag is that while other much-reprinted authors regularly have their 'look' redesigned, with new sets of uniform covers being commissioned and new artists' fees being paid, the Kirby Discworld covers are reckoned to be definitive. Corgi's 1993 experiment with a more restrained and 'upmarket' jacket for *The Colour of Magic*, painted by the talented Stephen Player, was unsuccessful. Thus the original Discworld covers appear on reprint after reprint but generate no further income for their creator. Artists are expected to maintain the noble tradition of starving in a garret. . .

CHAPTER TWO

MAGIC (UN)REALISM

In this section, many people who think they can infallibly recognize a Josh Kirby painting will find some surprises. His favourite comic-fantasy style may make him detectable when illustrating non-Discworld humour, but all is subtly changed when he approaches the lush and languid science fantasy of Robert Silverberg's 'Majipoor' stories.

Majipoor is a vast, exotic world where science and magic overlap under the rule of an ancient system of monarchy. In the first-written book, *Lord Valentine's Castle*, young Valentine has been defrauded of his memory and his Divine Right of Kings, and makes a journey of discovery through the world and up the colossal mountain of the Castle where he should be ruling. He duly claims the throne; the old, old story.

Kirby's cover picture shows us the immense coloured vistas of Majipoor, and artfully compresses the Castle mountain to a spindly pillar

Opposite:
Onward, Lord Valentine (c. 1982). The mysterious rider points us and Lord Valentine along the upward path to glory – and, recalling Longfellow's poem, carries a banner with a strange device. Kirby: 'Excelsior!'

Lord Valentine's Castle (1980; this cover Pan 1981) by Robert Silverberg. 'Designed to be a wrap-around,' says Kirby ruefully, 'but used in the first instance like a postage-stamp with the cover mostly lettering . . .

Valentine's Arch. A Majipoor cover that wasn't in fact used on a Silverberg book. Instead, Kirby recollects that 'much to Terry Pratchett's horror it was first used on a German edition of one of his'. In fact it was two of his: *Die Schiebenwelt* (Heyne 1994), containing *The Light Fantastic* and *Equal Rites.*

that somehow suggests truly vertiginous heights. A floating vehicle moves along the approach road. On closer examination the colours and textures, particularly of the floater and the mixed-species crowd following behind, are far more fluid, elusive and impressionistic than those of Discworld. From a certain distance, it's possible to be reminded of the strange textures seen in Max Ernst's surrealist landscape paintings *Europe After the Rain* (1942) and *The Eye of Silence* (1944).

Another, similar evocation of the tranquillized glories of Majipoor shows more of the floating craft emerging from odd arched structures against a beach and sea background. Kirby's title for this is *Valentine's Arch*; it was his first attempt at a *Lord Valentine's Castle* cover, which in the end wasn't used for the book and so hasn't previously appeared in Britain.

Onward, Lord Valentine was inspired by Valentine's upward quest – both physical and metaphorical. Again, this is its first appearance in print. Discworld excepted, Kirby finds Majipoor his favourite fictional playground in which to locate paintings, and produced this one for the simple joy of doing so. Retrospectively, it became a step on the way to his cover painting for *Majipoor Chronicles*, as featured on two Pan editions.

'When I paint for myself – uncommissioned – I tend to paint science fantasy subjects without humorous content . . . in the line of Robert Silverberg's *Lord Valentine's Castle* and my own *The Voyage of the Ayeguy*.' When asked if he has any hobbies besides painting, he has been known to reply: 'More painting.'

Illustrating the British paperback of the later Majipoor title *Valentine Pontifex*, Kirby seems to be reacting against the languorousness of Silverberg's narration. He picks a scene – the sighting of a group of 'sea-dragons' – which both the book itself and Jim Burns's airbrushed cover for the Gollancz hardback describe in terms of almost static awe at these enormous, majestic and slow-moving creatures. By contrast, Kirby pours vigorous energy into his painting: the dragons tower menacingly rather than just floating there, while Valentine's fleet tilts crazily on huge and dangerous seas, and disaster seems a distinct possibility.

As so often in Kirby's later work, this painting's curves and masses guide the eye to a distinct focal point at the right. The impressionistic, almost blurred treatment of the ship's bow in the foreground quietly prevents this from becoming a distraction. Overall it nicely illustrates this artist's fascination with a particular kind of spiral, which it's now time to examine more closely.

When interviewed, Kirby presents himself as an essentially *intuitive* artist, not one relying on or working by some elaborate theory of Art – and certainly not the Higher Art Criticism so ruthlessly satirized by Tom Wolfe in his polemic *The Painted Word* (1975). However, he's found many of his compositions unconsciously sharing a common factor whose theoretical underpinning he was delighted to hear about:

'The spiral that appears willy-nilly in my paintings was christened by a fan the KIRBY KURL KONSTANT. My attention was first drawn to it by a professor of art history, Dr Francis Litna, who called it the Danube spiral and explained that all art originating in the culture of the Danube basin had it. I was happy to see it in my own work and didn't resist its appearance, like a ghost at a wedding . . . .'

To mathematicians, this shape is a logarithmic spiral curve; to artists it's

Cover for 1985 Pan edition of *Valentine Pontifex* (1983) by Robert Silverberg. Majipoor has a two-tier monarchy, and in this book the time has come for Lord Valentine to give up his public 'Coronal' position and go into advisory seclusion as Pontifex after one last journey around the world.

a curve of growth that's found throughout nature in such places as spider-webs, the pattern of seeds in a sunflower head, and the shell of the nautilus. It links to another famous crossover between art and maths, the Golden Ratio or Golden Section, which is reckoned to be particularly aesthetically pleasing. A line is said to be divided in golden section if the shorter section of the line is to the longer one as the longer is to the whole line. From this you can work out the Golden Ratio mathematically (via a quadratic equation, omitted because in publishing lore each equation is said to halve a book's sales). This magic number is sometimes called *phi*; it goes on for infinitely many decimal places, and for practical mathematical purposes is about 1.618.

A golden rectangle is one whose long and short sides have lengths in this proportion. In real life, even three decimal places is probably overdoing the precision, and 'around 1.6' seems more sensible. So a 3-in x 5-in (8-cm x 13-cm) file card (ratio of sides 1.67) isn't far off being a golden rectangle; the now old-fashioned foolscap paper size at 8 in x 13 in (13 cm x 33 cm) comes closer (1.625); and the $18^3/_8$-in x $11^1/_2$-in (47-cm x 29-cm) canvas that Kirby uses for front-cover paintings is very close indeed.

The connection between golden rectangles and the Kirby Kurl Konstant appears in the 'whirling squares' diagram (left), based on the geometrical fact that if you divide a golden rectangle into two sections, one of which is square, the smaller section is another golden rectangle. This can be continued forever; and as the shapes get smaller and smaller, they trace out a logarithmic or Danube spiral.

As with the golden ratio, there's no need to get too mystical about the spiral. At its simplest the diagram suggests a rule of composition for paintings. Putting the main subject, the focus of the picture, at dead centre is boring. Things feel better when it's offset to roughly a golden-ratio

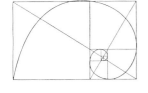

Above and below: These 'whirling squares' show the relationship between golden rectangles and a logarithmic spiral. (Based on a figure in Martin Gardner's *More Mathematical Puzzles and Diversions*, 1961.) Kirby was pleased and surprised to find that this magic spiral is so often echoed in his work and, as here, suggests the focal point of a picture.

Poster for the fantasy movie *Beastmaster* (1985), whose vaguely Conan- or Tarzan-like hero has the ability to communicate with various animals. Somehow Kirby managed to resist including the comic ferrets which also featured as conversational partners.

position, both horizontally and vertically, and this is where the spiral converges. On a wraparound cover it's particularly natural for the focus of the painting to be offset to the right rather than the left, since there's a certain commercial pressure to put the highlight on the front rather than the back cover. . .

So the Kirby or Danube spiral suggests the route along which the viewer's eye is led through a painting's internal 'story'. Although it's an imaginary line and certainly needn't feature explicitly, you can often trace sections of it in a Kirby composition – in, for example, that surging sea-scene from Robert Silverberg's *Valentine Pontifex* which was discussed above and appears on page 31. Here the spiral is echoed in the wave-shapes of the foreground and the curve of the sea-dragons' necks, gently guiding our eyes to the red sail which is the natural dramatic focus of this intensely alive painting.

A final, serious word from Kirby on this subject: 'I feel the Danube spiral links all Western art . . . It is an important heritage and I think it is part of the job of the artist to link with what has gone before and carry what is good in our civilization forward for future generations.'

Movie posters have very different design dynamics from book cover artwork, but Kirby's frequent comic-fantasy technique of combining images from many different scenes works usefully in this context. In *Beastmaster*, for example, the hero – who can talk with and understand animals – appears both at stage centre with appropriate beasties and in vignettes of swordplay. The slave girl whom he fancies is similarly doubled, presenting a rear view for fanciers of female buttocks plus a winsome about-to-be-sacrificed tableau at the right. And students of the deep grammar of

Top left:
The Panchronicon Plot (DAW 1977) – as indicated by
its title, Ron Goulart's comic SF novel features lots of derring-
do *via* time travel, echoed by Kirby's depictions of clothes from
different eras. Note the cheery reptilian aliens and their truly
terrible dress sense.

Far left, below:
The Other Side of the Sky (1958; this cover Corgi 1966), story collection by Arthur C. Clarke. A touch of Daliesque *trompe l'oeil* here: two metallic hands grasp what may be a metal heart, but the central 'arm bones' keep flickering in perception and becoming legs to match those of the almost humanoid figure at right. (Kirby on Dali: 'I like him.')

Above:
Poster for the third *Star Wars* movie, *Return of the Jedi* (1983). Has Princess Leia *noticed* how many variously cute entities are all standing on her long trailing dress?

Movie poster for *Monty Python's Life of Brian* (1979). Although this contains minutely detailed allusions to the film – even the painfully corrected Latin graffito ROMANI ITE DOMUM – Kirby subordinates everything to the huge citadel/title and thus he tactfully avoids foregrounding the Python team's highly controversial parallels with the life of Christ. This actually appeared only in the 1979 Python book of the film.

movie posters should find it quite easy to identify the evil high priest against whom the hero plans revenge.

The poster for *Return of the Jedi* is similarly crowded with now all too familiar *Star Wars* characters, this time shown with painstaking photographic realism in contrast to the slight fantastication of the *Beastmaster* figures. For *Monty Python's Life of Brian*, Kirby took a different line and merged Hollywood's 'huge letters of stone' title cliché with a gentle spoof of Bruegel's archetypal fantasy edifice *The Tower of Babel* (1566).

Also poster-like are the designs for the *Battlefield Earth* calendar, a promotional artefact that was part of the publicity overkill for L. Ron Hubbard's truly dreadful space opera *Battlefield Earth: A Saga of the Year 3000* (1982). Hubbard had written some interesting SF and fantasy in the 1940s, but after decades of getting rich as the founder of Scientology his return to the SF genre was sadly over-long and self-indulgent. The wicked and hissable alien appearing in both paintings is Terl the Psychlo (his race thus called as a dig at psychologists and psychiatrists, against whom Scientology has always waged a kind of religious war). This bad guy's characterization is perhaps best summed up in Hubbard's line: 'He went to sleep gloating over how clever he was.'

Decades earlier, the semi-abstract 1966 cover painting for Arthur C. Clarke's collection *The Other Side of the Sky* shows the influence of Richard Powers (1921–1996), whose idiosyncratic and non-representational SF covers had made a great impression on Kirby: 'The curious metal objects and sparkling flows of energy being interchanged in the Powers covers especially stimulated me.' Some version of the swirling patterns of force in

36

Above:
Battlefield Earth I (1983),
painted for a 1984 promo-
tional calendar whose theme
was L. Ron Hubbard's 1982
SF novel. Hero Jonnie
Goodboy Tyler triumphs
over alien villain Terl while
his girlfriend – whose part
in the story consists mainly
of bursting regularly into
tears – completes the composition.

Left:
Battlefield Earth III (1983),
unused design for 1984
promotional calendar. Here
nasty alien Terl has our hero
leashed, but one guesses it
won't be for long.

the background is quite often seen in Kirby's earlier SF painting, and the
strange, ambiguous foreground figure (or figures) is echoed in various later
SF objects which mingle organic and metallic qualities.

A less abstract example is the lushly curved Panchronicon – that is, a
fancy name for a time machine – on the cover of *The Panchronicon Plot*
(1977) by Ron Goulart. This sought-after plot device is described as resem-
bling 'a small, antique phone booth which had been decorated some with

Right:
Duelmaster: Arena of Death Book I (Collins/Armada 1987) by Mark Smith and Jamie Thomson. Designed to `join up' with the second gladiator painting for Book II. These two-player game-books came in pairs, one book for each player.

Far right:
Duelmaster: Arena of Death Book II (Collins/Armada 1987) by Mark Smith and Jamie Thomson. The lordly watcher above looks to be in a thumbs-down mood. . .

Facing page:
The Berlin Wall (1986; not previously published) draws on life experience during Kirby's Berlin exhibition, but was painted back at home with a postcard to jog his memory of the Wall. 'My host was much moved by its existence and he talked me into painting it. It made me nervous at the time as I thought the KGB might arrive to get me!'

chrome trim'. Which sounds a little dull and cuboidal, but didn't discourage Kirby from convoluting it into something rich and strange.

He is of course all too aware that his favourite SF and fantasy subjects prevent him from being taken seriously by any modern art critic: 'Critics are unable to make a connection between previous art forms and science fiction. SF/fantasy pulp magazines have formed a barrier with their air of the trivial and transient and infantile, and I think this makes many critics feel they must defend their dignity and reputation. Although the Greek myths and Bible stories that furnished the Renaissance artists (not to forget Bruegel and Bosch) with their subject matter are the direct ancestors of modern fantasy and SF, the connection is overlooked.'

Right:
Spaceman Rose – a surreal painting that become the cover for Damon Knight's anthology *A Century of Great Short Science Fiction Novels* (1964; this cover Mayflower 1970).

Far right:
Vanity of Duluoz (1968; this cover Quartet 1973) by Jack Kerouac . . . showing Kerouac himself as an angel-winged American footballer. 'About his person' – in Kirby's phrase – are fellow Beat-movement writers William S. Burroughs, Gregory Corso and Allen Ginsberg.

Perhaps more to critics' tastes is the touch of surrealism in the curious jux-tapositions found in the anthology cover for *A Century of Great Short Science Fiction Novels* – which Kirby calls *Spaceman Rose* – and in the composite figure of Jack Kerouac painted for a Quartet edition of Kerouac's *Vanity of Duluoz*. His picture for Robert Sheckley's *Untouched by Human Hands*, with an ordinary staircase displaced into a desert and leading only to nothingness, is regarded as a classic by SF cover connoisseurs. Its disorienting mix of the matter-of-fact and the bizarre recalls the blandly surreal paintings of René Magritte (1898–1967) – though Magritte's version of the scene would have been infinitely more static, transfixed in time. Kirby: 'I delight in Magritte's paradoxes.'

Conversely, the matched gladiator covers for the two volumes of *Arena of Death* (part of the 'Duelmaster' two-player gamebook series) use an almost painfully detailed hyper-realism in which every ornamental embossing or decoration of armour and weaponry is lingeringly dwelt on, like patterns seen in nightmare or delirium.

A small surprise after all these strange excursions is the previously unpublished painting *Balancing Nudes*, whose only fantastic aspect is its symmetry. Kirby is a little hazy about the genesis of this romantic design, but on reflection feels that 'I suppose I had Art Nouveau in mind at the time, which I think lies behind the general SF style to some extent'.

The Berlin Wall, also previously unpublished, is a genuine exercise in magic realism. Realism, since the Berlin Wall is as Kirby saw it while exhibiting his work in 1986 at the Hammer Gallery, Berlin. Magic, because he couldn't resist embellishing the grim concrete reality with fantastic symbols of death and evil flying above, of life and sexiness below. Can it be coincidence that after being Kirbified, the Wall was able to stand for only three more years? Well . . . possibly.

A final, bizarre indicator of Kirby's infiltration of popular culture is what he calls his *Fairground Side-Show Montage* – photographed from an actual funfair attraction that had been lavishly decorated with scaled-up copies of his work, with of course a cheery disregard for copyright. 'When that fairground mirror maze "Labyrinth" used my paintings from *In the Garden of Unearthly Delights*, I thought I must have "arrived" – I've been incorporated into folk art!'

Balancing Nudes (undated) is published here for the first time. Asked what inspired this unusual and charming image, Kirby is not afraid to say: 'I don't remember! I think I just wanted a small painting.'

Fairground Side-Show Montage (1990s): Kirby as folk art, photographed from real life by himself. 'All the side-shows were so jammed together I couldn't get back far enough, so thus a montage was all I could manage. I panicked the owner as he thought I was out for a copyright fee. . .'

CHAPTER THREE

THINGS THAT GO BUMP

Josh Kirby isn't generally associated with horror, violence or the darker side of the supernatural. Nevertheless he has produced covers for a good number of horror stories and collections. As a rule he prefers not to reprint or even to acknowledge the many bread-and-butter painting assignments for which he has had to conform to a conventional, art-editor view of spooky matters. Sometimes, though, he's been allowed to deal with spine-chilling subjects while retaining a healthy measure of Kirbyesque quirkiness, surrealism or general stylistic flourish.

One such opportunity came with a longish sequence of horror anthologies that traded on movie director Alfred Hitchcock's reputation as a master of fear. A typical title was *Alfred Hitchcock Presents . . . Stories They*

Above:
Murders I Fell in Love With (1969; this cover Mayflower 1974) . . . what interpretation of this Hitchcock title could improve on Kirby's delivery of a particularly pointed Valentine message? A lovesome thing, God wot.

Left:
Games Killers Play (1967; this cover Mayflower 1974) was the anthology title, and so we find the ultimate killer – Death himself – playing his own game with the cards that editor Hitchcock thought were merely for whiling away the time with Patience.

Above:
The title *Alfred Hitchcock's Death Bag* (1969; this cover Mayflower 1974) leads naturally enough to the image of portly Hitchcock as a dark Father Christmas shouldering a swollen bagful of death . . . the extra Kirby touch being that it looks as though one of the deaths in there may be Hitchcock's own.

Below left:
Yet another Hitchcock horror collection, *Meet Death at Night* (Four Square 1967), provided Kirby with an irresistible temptation to make the introduction suggested by the title, and lay Hitchcock out in state.

Wouldn't Let Me Do On TV. Most if not all of these were in fact ghost-edited for Hitchcock by such unsung figures as Robert Arthur (one of whose contributions was co-edited with SF author Thomas M. Disch), Harold Q. Masur and the very copious anthologist Peter Haining (whose recent comic-fantasy anthologies have all had Kirby covers – see Cosmic Capers and Discworld Revisited). Some stories were recycled several times in different Hitchcock-fronted collections, and it wasn't unknown for these collections to be blatantly reprinted with different titles to look like brand-new anthologies.

For these books, Kirby developed the looming image of Hitchcock as a genially evil MC who presided over his ghosts and nightmares like that comic-sinister storyteller the Crypt Keeper in the old EC horror comic *Tales from the Crypt*. It proved possible to take the mickey and inject sly humour at regular intervals. The fact that Hitchcock in later life was rather an obese fellow did not escape Kirby's eye.

Perhaps the funniest and most Kirbyish of these covers is for the anthology *Games Killers Play*, showing a bloated Hitchcock seated at a table laying out a game of Patience that turns into a fortune-telling spread. As he is slowly and a little nervously beginning to register, all the cards are Aces of Spades. Behind him, Death – not in Discworld robes but just bare bones – entices the reader into complicity with a grin and a bony finger touched to his lack of lips, as though saying: 'Ssssh! Don't spoil the surprise!'

Other wry paintings star Hitchcock in a variety of doom-laden situations which tend to erode his authority as MC of horror. They stow him away behind bars (*Bar the Doors*); lay him out in an expensive open coffin where his sleep seems strangely troubled (*Meet Death at Night*); show him ruefully examining the arrow that's pierced a heart-shaped red target on his shirt-front (*Murders I Fell in Love With*); place him in a graveyard

from which skeletons are erupting, either to the call of the Last Trump or because large movie directors are tasty (*Rolling Gravestones*); burden him with a sinister sack that seems to be fighting back (*Death Bag*); and show him propping up his weary head with one hand – a hand that on second glance isn't human (*A Month of Mystery*).

Of course, it's possible that this gentle spoofing and distancing of Hitchcock's horrors was a form of self-defence. In one unguarded moment Kirby has admitted: 'Hitchcock was in fact a bit too real for me. I was terrified by *Psycho*. Luckily showers hadn't been invented in England then.'

Returning again and again to the same central character seems like a recipe for staleness, but Kirby kept happily ringing the changes on Hitchcock. For more than one painting (*A Month of Mystery*, *Stories to be Read with the Lights On*, and the unpublished *Hitchcock With Cigar*) he adapted the favourite technique of Milanese painter Guiseppe Arcimboldo (1527–1593). Arcimboldo liked to build up surreally disturbing images of faces or heads from painted assemblies of fruit, vegetables, birds or animals. Although Kirby also used various beasts as Hitchcock components, his neatest twist was to construct the familiar Hitchcock face from traditional images of horror. Turn back to the Biographical Introduction for paintings in which a similar treatment is administered to that terrifying figure of nightmare, Terry Pratchett.

Arcimboldo's approach also inspired the cover for Colin Wilson's strange philosophical porn novel *The God of the Labyrinth*, in which a classic satyr-head – emblem of lust – is assembled from writhing, naked female bodies. Indeed, this construction of a grotesque from seeming 3-D objects is much closer to the Arcimboldo technique than Kirby's subtler overlaying of imagery on a normally shaped Hitchcock face.

Above:
For Hitchcock's *Rolling Gravestones* (1971; this cover Mayflower 1974), one suspects the editor imagined the tombstones falling with slow, sinister suspense. Instead, our artist impishly supplies a scene of demonic energy, with only Hitchcock himself placidly becalmed in this seething graveyard.

Left:
A Month of Mystery (1969; this UK edition Pan 1973 in 2 volumes) – does this particular Hitchcock's right hand know what his left hand doeth?

Facing page, right:
Bar the Doors (1965; this cover Mayflower 1974), a Hitchcock anthology extracted from an earlier and fatter 1946 volume with the same title. Similar thrifty recycling was rampant through the series. Horror fans would often find they'd bought an old collection under a new title, and probably did want to put the culprit behind bars.

Right:
Hitchcock with Cigar . . .
even Josh Kirby can't trace
the publication of this
Illustrated Man-like
Hitchcock painting with the
added secret ingredient of a
big cigar. He suspects that it
may never have been used.

Below:
The God of the Labyrinth
(1970; this cover Mayflower
1971) by Colin Wilson is an
eccentric novel in which
Wilson uses pornographic
conventions as a route to
his repeated dream of
Nietzschean transcendence
via intense imaginative
exertion, here of course
achieved through orgasm.
A difficult book to illustrate
for a family publisher. . .

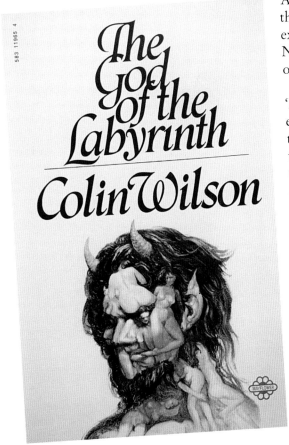

Kirby himself suspects that this particular orgiastic theme may owe more to feelthy postcards than direct Old Master influence: 'Arcimboldo is of course the source of the Hitchcock heads, though I came to it by a devious route before I knew of his existence, via my brother finding a French postcard of Napoleon's head made of nudes – it made a great impression on my young mind.' Well, it would, wouldn't it?

Another inspiration was perhaps a little less obvious: 'Ray Bradbury's *Illustrated Man* had a seminal influence. It excited me and inspired me and led me into painting portraits with much more happening in the faces, apart from the likeness. More illustrated men, in fact. Ghosts and fantasies, witches and images from the dark night of the imagination parading for those who wish to see . . . I did a whole series of heads of Alfred Hitchcock in this way.'

Kirby has remarked that he doesn't as a rule use artists' models or lay figures, but often draws from found objects: 'I invent the images, then see if I can find natural objects to draw from: people, vehicles, rocks and so on. If I don't draw I take photographs for reference or look for pictures in magazines. I will use anything that helps.' The sinister ultra-realism of *The Severed Hand*, painted for Guy de Maupassant's story of the same title, is likely to be based on his own hand – with, one hopes, exaggerated fingernails. Likewise, 'I use a mirror sometimes for eyes, ears, etcetera.' Discworld fans have often believed they can actually see Kirby's face among the Bruegel-like background crowds on some Pratchett

44

1969 Panther Books cover for *The Chinese Bell Murders* by Robert van Gulik (1958). This and other 'Judge Dee' novel covers were painted as details rather than filled canvases: a central image that gains strength from appearing against a pure white background on the jacket. Although Kirby prefers to create a complete, framable picture when painting Discworld, here he agreed with this approach and was 'rather pleased with the overall look'.

covers, but the artist says that any resemblance is accidental.

With another change of style, Kirby produced some striking 'Oriental' paintings for 1969 editions of Robert van Gulik's historical detective stories based on the exploits of the seventh-century Chinese magistrate Judge Dee. Dee was a genuine historical figure, whose reputation as a solver of crimes led to his becoming the hero of much later Chinese crime fiction. The Chinese thriller convention of supplying clues and information via ghosts or revenants, though downplayed by van Gulik, added enough fantastic *frisson* to attract Kirby.

A huge old temple bell features prominently in *The Chinese Bell Murders*, and Kirby depicts this with great realism but juggles with detail to

Right:
Robert van Gulik's *The Chinese Maze Murders* (1962; this cover 1969) features a literal maze as well as a grisly labyrinth of multiple investigations for Chinese magistrate Judge Dee – so the painting is doubly symbolic. One unfortunate girl is indeed beheaded in the book.

Below:
The Night Side (1947; this cover Four Square 1966), a creepy collection assembled by August Derleth, carries Kirby's version of the head of Medusa – the Gorgon with the petrifying gaze, indicated by making her eyes very odd indeed. Either that, or having one's head cut off by a Hero leads to a severe and visible hangover.

provide a striking rather than an entirely accurate image of violence. It is a skeleton and not a fresh corpse which Judge Dee discovers hidden under the ancient bell, which in fact is large enough to trap Dee's entire party of five investigators when the lurking villain knocks away the props that held it temporarily tilted up . . . but that bloodied hand would lose effectiveness if drawn to scale.

When painting his cover for *The Chinese Maze Murders* Kirby opted for surreal symbolism, making van Gulik's outdoor maze of trees and swamp into something artificial and iconic, extending through space and defying gravity – its bizarreness contrasting with the meticulous portraits of Judge Dee himself in his magistrate's regalia. An obvious nod here is to works by M.C. Escher (1898–1971): *Another World* (wood-engraving, 1947) and *Relativity* (lithograph, 1953), each featuring three intersecting realities where gravity operates in different directions. Perhaps Kirby missed a trick by increasing the number of 'down' directions from three, which would have echoed the book's three intertwined plots (it was a realistic aspect of the old Chinese thriller tradition that magistrates investigated three simultaneous cases). He remembers: 'I so admired Escher, and he was much in the air at that time; I do tend to reflect my current enthusiasms.'

All the Judge Dee covers carry an artist's credit, but to Ron Kirby rather than Josh Kirby. This arose because David Larkin, the Panther

Far left:
A Stir of Echoes (1958; this cover Corgi 1965). The woman/skull face symbolizes the telepathic clues from beyond the grave that both complicate and eventually unravel Richard Matheson's strange murder mystery.

Left:
The Rack. In this cover for the anonymously edited Corgi anthology *Black Tales* (1965), Kirby uses aerial perspective to show a famous piece of mediaeval fitness equipment at – as it were – full length.

Books art editor at that time, knew him only as Ron. As Kirby mysteriously remarks, 'I had to use my birth name to get an official job though I'd been known by my nickname Josh for years by all my friends.' His European agent seems to have the same preference for a 'real' birth name: recent French and Hungarian editions of Terry Pratchett novels have likewise credited the covers to Ron Kirby.

Another, earlier novel of spooky violence, Richard Matheson's *A Stir of Echoes*, inspired an energetic cover which mixes techniques. The central portrait of a partly skeletal woman's face is a familiar image of horror, but appears against – or is breaking through – a more stylized background of jumbled coloured cuboids. In Matheson's story, a dead woman's mind does indeed seem to be breaking through into the living world to issue the hero with psychic clues that lead very tortuously to her own murderer.

Other more or less conventional horror props appear in anthology covers for the anonymously edited *Black Tales*, with a torture chamber and rack; for August Derleth's *The Night Side*, featuring the uncomfortable gaze of Medusa; and for *The Unquiet Grave* – also edited by Derleth – where robed, bony figures who seem to be the King and Queen of Terrors welcome a revenant as he rises from his open grave. Yet another skeleton, of some unfortunate who has fallen prey to hidden danger in the jungle, features on the cover painting for Geoffrey Household's *The Dance of the Dwarfs*. This painting reminds us again that Kirby can paint with near-photographic realism when so inclined . . . though his personal inclinations tend elsewhere.

The brutish figure of Mr Hyde, from Robert Louis Stevenson's classic chiller *Strange Case of Dr Jekyll and Mr Hyde*, has become an icon of horror who hardly needs to be captioned. Like the ever-popular bogeymen Dracula, Frankenstein's monster and the Phantom of the Opera, Hyde is instantly recognizable – as his nice but unwise alter ego Dr Jekyll is not. In this story of terrible transformations Stevenson said something enduring about the dark side of the human spirit, or at least about how we like

Right:
Kirby's title for this grim graveyard scene is *After Doré*. It became a cover for August Derleth's anthology *The Unquiet Grave* (1964; this cover Four Square, 1968).

Far right:
The Dance of the Dwarfs (1968; this cover Mayflower 1971). In this novel by Geoffrey Household – best known for *Rogue Male* (1938) – toting a gun may still not save you from the feral horrors in the Amazon jungle.

Below:
The Severed Hand (1973), the cover painting for *Tales of Supernatural Terror* (1969 compilation in French as *Contes du Surnaturel*, translated 1972) by Guy de Maupassant. Naturally this was inspired by de Maupassant's grisly story with the same title.

Overleaf:
Charles Maturin's antihero *Melmoth the Wanderer* (1820; this cover Four Square 1966) is one of the fellows which the 1997 *Encyclopedia of Fantasy* had in mind in its theme entry on 'Accursed Wanderers'. When the disgraced Oscar Wilde – Maturin's great-nephew – left prison and went into exile, he adopted the name Sebastian Melmoth.

to imagine it. Kirby's version of Hyde follows conventional lines, but understates the horror by making him a merely troubling figure in an atmospherically foggy and gaslit street . . . until a closer look reveals the bestiality of the face.

Here the publishers' art editor decided to eliminate any such shilly-shallying attempts at subtlety, and zoomed in on Hyde to highlight his obvious dental problems. Compare Kirby's painting with the final cover design, which actually uses less than 10 per cent of the original.

Last in this selection of horrific and violent pictures comes the accursed antihero of Charles Maturin's Gothic classic *Melmoth the Wanderer*. Melmoth has bought extended life at the price of his soul, which is why he looks very considerably doomed. Indeed, as with those sly Hitchcock paintings, there's a sense here that Kirby has his tongue in his cheek and is enjoying himself hugely by laying on the Gothic elements with a trowel. Not only is Melmoth expressing Byronic Angst with all the projective power of a silent movie star, but there's the (rather more cheery-looking) skull that he's clutching, the Gothic castellations behind, the electrical storm splitting the whole sky, the toppling tower struck by lightning. . . .

Nothing exceeds like excess.

Collectors of Kirby's paperback work have a number of further horror titbits to seek out in old British editions – including story collections by Robert Bloch, Mary Elizabeth Counselman, Gerald Kersh, Arthur Machen and Richard Matheson, a Four Square edition of William Beckford's perverse Arabian horror-fantasy *Vathek*, and creepy anthologies edited by Peter Haining, Dashiell Hammett and Kurt Singer. Kirby's own checklist of completed book-cover paintings (that he's prepared to acknowledge!) appears as an appendix to this book on page 104.

Left:
Strange Case of Dr Jekyll and Mr Hyde (painted 1973). Robert Louis Stevenson's Mr Hyde, the drug-evoked dark side of nice Dr Jekyll, needs no introduction. The story of dreadful transformation emerged from a genuine nightmare suffered by the author.

Below:
Strange Case of Dr Jekyll and Mr Hyde II (1886; this cover New English Library 1974). Here we see some of the games publishers play: using a mere expanded detail of Kirby's full-length painting, and getting the title wrong. Stevenson's original title contains no 'The'.

The New English Library Classic Novel Series

THE STRANGE CASE OF Dr. JEKYLL AND Mr. HYDE
Robert Louis Stevenson

CHAPTER FOUR

COSMIC CAPERS

Rather as Stephen King's enormous success revitalized the flagging horror
market for many years, the permanent bestseller status of Terry Pratchett's
Discworld in Britain has – in combination with the solid if less spectacular
popularity of Tom Holt and Robert Rankin in particular – greatly raised the
profile of humorous fantasy and made it a popular subgenre. Josh Kirby
naturally approves:

'I like humour! Introducing humour into fantasy lightens the mood in
a pleasing way and allows a more playful approach to painting covers, so I
am glad about this development.'

It follows that with Kirby jackets established as virtually the trademark
image of Pratchett and thus of British comic fantasy bestsellers, several
optimistic publishers have commissioned paintings in the same vein to
boost other books of comic or would-be-comic fantasy. This section offers

Below left:
A 'double-exposure' view of
the opening scene in Tom
Holt's *Expecting Someone
Taller* (1987; this cover
Futura 1991). Ingolf appears
first as the run-over badger
and then in his true Frost
Giant form – Kirby eco-
nomically telescopes time
and superimposes the two.

Below right:
Another and particularly
frenetic Kirby 'action
tableau' is the centrepiece of
this cover for *Six Days*
(Kingsway 1992), a humorous
SF novel by Nick Page.

Who's Afraid of Beowulf? (1988; this reissue Orbit 1991) by Tom Holt. The small 'chthonic spirits' Zxerp and Prexz are described only as faint pools of light in the text – an opportunity for Kirby to imagine shapes for them and tuck them under the sorcerer's arm.

a selection of paintings which are all in the artist's familiar, lush style – but are set in worlds other than Discworld.

Tom Holt is probably the funniest author to have received this treatment; interestingly, he works in a distinct and indeed an older tradition of humour. Most modern comic fantasy takes place in some version of Fantasyland, that generic setting whose features have been pinched from J.R.R. Tolkien (above all), William Morris, Fritz Leiber and Robert E. Howard of Conan fame, with a smidgeon of Jack Vance and a dash of Disney. Fantasyland is packed with elves, dwarfs, orcs, dragons, trolls, wizards, heroes, faithful companions, castles, taverns, miscellaneous monsters in profusion, rolling hills, underground labyrinths, Forests and Mountains of Doom, and one Dark Lord. Square mountain ranges are a frequent geographical oddity. We all know it by heart; it's cruelly anatomized in Diana Wynne Jones's very funny *The Tough Guide to Fantasyland* (1996).

Holt, though, prefers the real Earth as his setting, and tends to inject a bracing dose of fantasy into mundane life – like Sir W .S. Gilbert unleashing a fairy horde on Parliament in *Iolanthe* (first performed 1882), or F. Anstey afflicting his staid Victorian hero with a too-helpful genie in *The Brass Bottle* (1900). His first comic fantasy, *Expecting Someone Taller*, lands wimpy-but-nice hero Malcolm with the Ring of Wagnerian legend, giving him power over all Earth – to the horror of unreconstructed gods like Wotan (Odin) who find the world becoming inexorably happier and nicer. Malcolm's mere unconscious influence improves every aspect of life on Earth except the one evil which is utterly irreparable, the English cricket team's Test Match performance.

Kirby's cover shows the opening scene in which Malcolm, having run over a badger in his car, is briefed on the awesome fact that he has just dealt a mortal blow to Ingolf, last of the Frost Giants and custodian of the Tarnhelm and the Ring, who happened to be in shapeshifted disguise. Evidence of the wealth-generating power of the Ring is strewn around, and news of what's happened will very shortly reach Wotan since his ravens Thought and Memory – better known as Hugin and Munin – are watching nervously. Ingolf is surely just in the process of remarking, as do other characters on first meeting the new Ring-master, that he was expecting someone taller. . .

The magical irruption into the world in Holt's nicely titled *Who's Afraid of Beowulf?* is a longshipful of Norsemen who awaken from 1,200 years' enchanted slumber to be singularly unimpressed by modern technology.

Any forbidden official doorway may open into the dungeons of the dread Chastel des Larmes Chaudes in Tom Holt's *Overtime* (Orbit 1993) – including, it seems, the door of a pillar-box through which Blondel here sees a past or future Blondel slipping. Time travel is fraught with such tangles.

Ye Gods! (Orbit 1992) by Tom Holt. Slightly skewed versions of Jupiter (with thunderbolt), Minerva (with owl), Mercury (with winged hat) and other gods and centaurs are grouped around the colossal chained figure of Prometheus – who will not stay imprisoned much longer, now that a Hero is on the way.

They have magic stones and enchanted armour that can do as much or better, after all: here they're seeing off a copter-load of police and BBC film crew, while a wolf, a sorcerer and the archaeologist heroine look on. A crowded composition conveys the book's episodic, anarchic fun.

Further Tom Holt illustrations followed. In *Flying Dutch*, the true story of Vanderdecker the legendary Flying Dutchman is exposed: he and his crew drank an elixir of life which gave them immortality, invulnerability and a terrible stench that forces them to put as much sea-room as possible between their accursed ship *Verdomde* and civilization. Kirby took up the challenge to cram rather more of the globe than would seem possible into this wraparound cover (see page 7).

Secret portals through time and space – which according to Holt are what lie behind the ubiquitous official doors marked NO ENTRY in every era – complicate the task of Richard Lionheart's legendary singer Blondel in *Overtime*. His search for his imprisoned king ramifies across time and becomes a mad chase involving assassins, antipopes and the Antichrist. More than once the action passes through a prison cell whose anonymous occupant is Richard himself, thus making his forlorn appearance at the left of the painting wittily accurate. The game of Holt's *Ye Gods!* is to inflict a Hero on dull suburbia: young Jason Derry, who even at the age of three is hauling vast slain or captured animals home to his mortal Mum and Dad. It's in the blood, since like Hercules, Jason is a bastard son of Jupiter/ Zeus... Prometheus and half the classical pantheon of gods get mixed up in the story.

(Later Holt jackets used other artists and a distinctive white-backgrounded design, sending the message that Holt is far from being a Pratchett clone. Since Gollancz adopted their mostly white hardback covers at around the same time, some fans naughtily suggested that the Discworld books were being rebranded to look like Tom Holt's...)

As Holt remarks in his introduction to this collection, the 'Kirbyization' of humorous authors has become almost a cliché of genre publishing. Craig Shaw Gardner, an American fantasy writer who has been somewhat less successful in Britain (just as Terry Pratchett used to have a much lower profile in the USA), was duly spin-doctored in this way as

Craig Shaw Gardner's *Revenge of the Fluffy Bunnies* (Headline 1990) concludes his 'Cineverse' cycle, whose conceit is that alternate fantasy worlds correspond to hackneyed movie scenarios. Kirby responds appropriately to this mix of deliberate clichés, slapstick and cliffhangers by showing the wizard (in particular) in more simplified and cartoon-like lines than usual.

Traditional fragments of Arabian fantasy litter this painting for Craig Shaw Gardner's *A Bad Day for Ali Baba* (Headline 1991) ... including a well-built if not entirely co-operative-looking houri, much gold, exotic headgear, minaret domes in the distance, and large jars suitable for 40 thieves to hide in.

Above:
Bizarre doings in the bazaar as Kirby enjoys himself with another crowded, minutely detailed chase sequence featuring a cast of thousands. *Scheherazade's Night Out* (Headline 1992) concludes Craig Shaw Gardner's trio of spoof Arabian Nights fantasies.

Far left:
Craig Shaw Gardner's *Raven Walking* (Reed 1994) opens the intentionally non-humorous Dragon Circle sequence. When wizards can't be identified by a pointy hat or mystic robes, streamers of magical force emerging from their fingertips may sometimes give the game away.

Left:
Dragon Waking (Reed 1995) by Craig Shaw Gardner is the second in this author's Dragon Circle sequence. The 'what happens next?' tension of fantastic art is here melodramatically strong.

Hooray for Hellywood (1990; this cover 1992) by Esther Friesner. All the horrors of Hell: ugly demons both male and female, skeletal demons, one-eyed demons (not to mention a monocular demon cat), and a pair of rather sexy succubi for variety. Obscure Discworld fact: the working title of Terry Pratchett's *Moving Pictures* was *Hooray for Holy Wood*.

writing Discworld lookalikes. Kirby's cover for the first Gardner novel *A Malady of Magicks* – not included here – precisely and perhaps slyly pointed up the contrast between Pratchett's polished humour and Gardner's more slapstick efforts by accurately depicting, just as in the book, the silly image of a tap-dancing dragon who sports a green top hat.

That painting contained another artistic influence which Kirby acknowledges: that of Arthur Rackham (1867–1939), the classic illustrator of fairies, goblins, elves and – almost his trademark image – wonderfully gnarled trees with humanlike facial features in their bark. For the first Gardner cover, Kirby had specifically tried to model his overall composition on Rackham in hope of signalling that this differed from the Discworld jackets he was doing for Gollancz and Corgi. But now he ruefully says: 'No one noticed the difference! And Gollancz were still annoyed . . .'

More slapstick followed in Gardner's 'Cineverse' trio, represented here by the chillingly titled *Revenge of the Fluffy Bunnies*. By the time of his spoof 'Arabian Nights' trilogy, Gardner's comedy had become smoother and more intricately imagined. The second volume, *A Bad Day for Ali Baba*, involves Ali Baba and Aladdin in the adventures of Sinbad (but the wrong Sinbad) that had begun in book one. With proper Arabian Nights recomplication, the first two stories emerge as being Sinbad's and Ali Baba's entries in a storytelling competition; the third volume is Scheherazade's effort, and as the teller of the tales in the original *Thousand and One Nights* she relates not only the story but the tale of how she's telling it. The complications and possibilities of getting lost amid the levels of story-telling, which become terrifying in Robert Irwin's 1983 dream-fantasy *The Arabian Nightmare*, are here well controlled and sunnily enjoyable.

The next Craig Shaw Gardner sequence, known as the 'Dragon Circle' books, is intentionally not humorous. Its sprawling plot features various people from our world who find new lives and new outlooks in a magical Fantasyland. Humorous or not, Kirby still tackles the covers with a verve that always threatens to bubble over into comedy. A raven naturally features in the foreground of his complex painting for *Raven Walking*. The next book, *Dragon Waking*, is represented by a similarly tight-packed indoor scene, interestingly showing some of the same highly recognizable characters in a new predicament and so teasing us (if we haven't yet read the novels) into imagining intervening fragments and links of story.

Esther Friesner is another US fantasy author whose work Kirby both likes and likes to illustrate. She's represented here by the painting for *Hooray for Hellywood*, the third volume of her very broadly comic 'Demons' trilogy. This is an exceedingly lightweight romp involving demons and Hollywood (of course), a dodgy TV evangelist, reincarnation, some excessively Californian Californians, and an excursion to Hell which clearly caught our artist's fancy.

Some authors never quite took off despite the boon of one or more Kirby covers. The covers were probably the best thing about Dan McGirt's 'Jason Cosmo' trilogy, whose hero blundered about a Fantasyland landscape of not-quite-funny placenames (Lower Hicksnittle, the Festering Wart Tavern, the Incredibly Dark Forest) and sank from sight after his third out-ing in *Dirty Work*, pictured here. Nick Page's comic SF novel *Six Days* seems to have been a one-off; Christopher Moore followed up his Californian fantasy *Practical Demonkeeping* with more horror-comedies that didn't perhaps seem suited to Kirby jackets.

Surprisingly, Kirby wasn't asked to illustrate British editions of *Good Omens*, Terry Pratchett's and Neil Gaiman's elaborate spoof of the *Omen* films in a very English setting. The initial concept was Gaiman's and involved replacing the demon child of the movies with the irrepressible William from Richmal Crompton's popular children's books. Indeed the working title was *William the Antichrist*, but the Crompton estate didn't quite see eye to eye with this, and names were changed. Kirby's chance came with the German edition, whose cover centrepiece is the guardian demon Crowley in full motorized flight over London. The Four Horsemen have here become four bikers (with a female redhead War, and Pestilence replaced by Pollution); the unknown and unwilling Antichrist, with his hellhound and gang of young delinquents, appears at left.

Armoured superhero Jason Cosmo has a spot of bother with the giant Demon Lord Asmodraxas and his mighty sword Daiquirimaker in Dan McGirt's less than overwhelmingly funny *Dirty Work* (Pan 1993).

Practical Demonkeeping (Mandarin 1992) by Christopher Moore. In this mildly comic fantasy, a demon is loosed in California . . . leading to the natural speculation, 'Well, who would notice?'

Facing page:
*Only You Can Save
Mankind* (1992; Het
Spectrum, Netherlands,
1994) by Terry Pratchett.
For some unknown reason
the British publisher of this
first book about young
Johnny Maxwell's escapades
didn't commission a Kirby
cover – but the Dutch had
different ideas.

Below:
Good Omens (1990; this
cover Heyne, Germany,
1997) by Terry Pratchett
and Neil Gaiman was translated into German with the
title's plural omens inexplicably becoming singular: *Ein
Gutes Omen*. Since Gaiman
was at the time far more
famous than Pratchett in the
USA, North American
editions of *Good Omens*
put his name first.

Pratchett's more science-fictional 'Johnny' books likewise acquired Kirby covers only in later, foreign editions. Johnny Maxwell's bizarre adventures begin in *Only You Can Save Mankind*, when the alien hordes in a shoot-'em-up computer game take him aback by surrendering and insisting that he escort them through 'game space' to safety – defending them en route from other human aggressors playing the same game. The painting shows an awkward moment when diffident Johnny and an all-too-macho girl acquaintance have entered game space and boarded the aliens' mothership. In the darker *Johnny and the Bomb*, our hero and his pals discover that the elderly local bag-lady Mrs Tachyon holds the key to a loophole through time, leading back to a particularly deadly day when the bombers came over in 1941.

Earlier Pratchett SF novels, written before Discworld saw print, were inevitably repackaged with romping Kirby covers in later years. *The Dark Side of the Sun*, an enjoyable space opera with both grim and comic episodes, features a variety of odd beasts and extraterrestrials which allowed Kirby to spread himself by inventing a selection of exotic grotesques. But as J.G. Ballard has remarked, the truly alien planet is Earth, and there's almost equal grotesquerie in the domestic chickens that star in Pratchett's brief 'Hollywood Chickens' squib, the basis for the cover of Peter Haining's anthology *Knights of Madness*.

Further excursions into comic SF rather than fantasy painting appeared

A little old lady's super-market trolley contains the secret of timeslipping between the present day and 1941 England in Terry Pratchett's third Johnny Maxwell book *Johnny and the Bomb* (1998; this edition Wahlström Bokforlag, Sweden, ? 1999).

on 1990s reissues of Harry Harrison's *The Technicolor Time Machine* and *Star Smashers of the Galaxy Rangers*. The first is (of course) a time-travel romp in which an ailing movie outfit travels back to film the 11th-century Viking discovery of America; archaeologists are later perplexed by the discovery of an empty bourbon bottle in a Norse midden-heap in Newfoundland. The second is a relentlessly over-the-top parodic assault on the crude but once beloved SF excesses of the 1930s 'Golden Age' – those pre-World War II days of ghastly innocence, when multiple genocide still seemed a nifty way to solve the problem of all those danged alien green-skins out there.

Left:
The Dark Side of the Sun II (Corgi 1993) by *Terry Pratchett*. The 1988 Corgi paperback had a different Kirby illustration; this replacement also appeared on the 1994 Doubleday hardback. Yes, after an assassination attempt which led to most of his body being regrown from greenish 'googoo' jelly, the human hero really *is* green.

Below:
Kirby's cover for the Peter Haining anthology *Knights of Madness: Further Comic Tales of Fantasy* (Souvenir 1998) illustrates the short Pratchett story 'Hollywood Chickens' – a joke piece which poses the classic question of how, using fowl-play technology and poultry power-sources, these chickens managed to cross the road.

Left:
Alan Dean Foster's *Quozl*
(1989; this cover New
English Library 1993), a
painting which brought
Kirby a complimentary
postcard from the author –
expressing huge relief that,
for the first time in his
career, the cover of a Foster
book actually represented
what he'd written.

Alan Dean Foster's comic SF novel *Quozl* is a slightly odd period piece, dealing with extraterrestrial visitors who – as Kirby faithfully shows – not only breed like rabbits but *look* like rabbits. They seek refuge on Earth and have the bad luck to arrive during World War II. In this scene of contact with a representative of humanity, Kirby has had huge fun with the stuffed animals decorating a hunting lodge. The staring stag's head over the door is all by itself a disturbance of the peace. Tilting the whole scene to the right boosts the ambience of crazy activity and confusion.

Book-cover paintings are subject to all sorts of constraints. They need to be 'readable' even at paperback-cover size, which can hamper Kirby's love of teeming detail. The right-hand half of a wraparound design has to make sense on its own. Space must be left empty or at least uncrowded for title and author information – the top third of a picture is the usual area for this, and outdoor scenes routinely include plenty of sky up there. For posters and stand-alone paintings, such rules don't apply.

Thus *Canute* is a simple and self-explanatory picture of King Canute or Cnut in his most famous pose: failing to hold back the oncoming tide by sheer force of majesty. This is occasionally told as a story of overweening pride deflated by Nature, but the more plausible version – that is, the better story – has flattering courtiers crediting their monarch with sea-repellent powers, and Canute himself insisting on a practical demonstration that time and tide wait for no king. Hence Kirby shows him looking back at the unseen watchers with an expression that seems to be saying, 'I *told* you so!'

The crammed, glowing, horrific-sensual detail of *The Four Deadly Riders* is at the other extreme of complexity. Commissioned by an American fan with a specific vision, it provided a challenge that took Kirby through many roughs before they reached agreement. 'He wanted a sort of amalgamation of the Four Horsemen of the Apocalypse and the Seven Deadly Sins – naturally, me being innumerate, this was no problem. . . He wanted Chaos, Lust, Hate and Madness.' And, indeed, there they are.

On a similarly lavish scale are the *Voyage of the Ayeguy* paintings, Josh Kirby's favourite private project, to which he has returned again and again for decades – a series of truly sumptuous images which outline the story of

Facing page, top:
*The Technicolor Time
Machine* by Harry
Harrison (1967; this edition
Orbit 1991) confronts
method-acting Vikings –
that chap on the cover is
really *projecting* berserkness
– with a time-shifted
Hollywood crew hoping to
film the discovery of
America by Erik the Red.
('Kill that idea! You want to
get us blacklisted with a
commie picture?')
Harrison's 'vremeatron'
time machine, a platform
mounted on thick insula-
tors, is accurately depicted.

Facing page, below:
Harry Harrison's *Star
Smashers of the Galaxy
Rangers* (1973; this edition
Orbit 1992) is a broad, no-
holds-barred, no-joke-too-
awful-to-use parody of SF
old-timer E.E. 'Doc' Smith's
Skylark books, in which
clean-cut, all-American
heroes purge the galaxy of
non-cuddly alien races.
Who, of course, lust after
our womenfolk.

Following pages:
The Four Deadly Riders II
(1996), based on a special
commission that later
became a poster by Clouded
Tiger Cards and also one of
a 1981 set of 16 postcards,
though never a cover. Very
unusually, Kirby parted with
the original (reproduced in
*In The Garden of Unearthly
Delights*), and created this
second version: 'As I feel
the need to hold on to my
originals I decided to paint
it again, to have and to hold
as it were. It is similar but
not quite the same, as
always happens when I redo
paintings.'

Right:
Canute. . . a '1981-ish' painting produced for an advertising agency on behalf of Newton Chambers Engineering Ltd, whose products and services (Kirby happily forgets the details) were evidently represented as a tide that couldn't be held back.

Below:
Go Civilize the Savage Planets II – an early (in terms of internal chronology) painting in the *Voyage of the Ayeguy* sequence, completed for Kirby's exhibition at the Williamson Art Gallery, Birkenhead, 1996, and not previously published. Using science-fantasy imagery, the tale of the Ayeguy echoes the mission, death and resurrection of Christ in the New Testament.

a kind of science-fictional messiah, his mission to spread enlightenment, his resulting death at the hands of the fearful and ignorant Imag, and what (as in every messiah story) comes after. Initially released as a 1981 portfolio of just six paintings, the sequence has been expanded over the years; at present there are 14. Oddly enough, a detail from one of these pictures turned up as the wholly inappropriate cover on a German edition of one of Terry Pratchett's Discworld novels.

Go Civilize the Savage Planets shows us the Ayeguy – the life-affirmer – being pointed on his way by a bearded father- or God-figure, awesomely robed and throned, against a background which is both futuristic and pastoral. We see the hero's spaceship, the *Ark*, awaiting in a launch-pad out on the green peninsula. Various Kirbyesque aliens are present, as well as a scatter of human onlookers.

In *Behold the Spaceman!*, our hero – with considerable supporting cast – shows himself to the masses on the porch or balcony of a particularly Kirby-styled building or temple. Its organic curves, seamed surface and purely decorative pointy bits were prefigured in several SF cover paintings to be found in the Future Fantastic section of this book.

Kirby continues to paint more *Voyage of the Ayeguy* pictures as time permits. From an April 1999 letter: 'I'm painting an Ayeguy picture right now – it's a larger version of *Resurrection* as in *Unearthly Delights*. So the series goes on; it might wind down, but no sign of that yet. . .' This is the longest-running of all his personal projects, and the dearest to his heart.

Behold the Spaceman! – another *Voyage of the Ayeguy* painting, completed in 1997. The BBC filmed Kirby at work on this picture, for the schools programme Arts Classics 3. All the paintings in this messianic sequence have a special, personal importance to him.

CHAPTER FIVE

FUTURE FANTASTIC

Terry Pratchett's joke about Josh Kirby being a Methuselah figure arose from the discovery, surprising to many people, that so many favourite SF paperback covers from decades ago turn out to be by Kirby. In Pratchett's words, 'Anyone with a decent collection of 50s/60s SF has a number of Josh Kirby covers already (in all sorts of styles). We ended up creating a sort of mythology that he'd been illustrating throughout the entire history of SF, which he plays up to with comments like "Has that nice young man Mr Wells written anything lately?" and mutterings that London looks completely different since they did away with the trams.'

Indeed Josh Kirby's first literary love was straight science fiction – fantasy simply wasn't recognized as a publishing genre in the 1950s, and a dark fantasy like Ray Bradbury's *Something Wicked This Way Comes* had to be packaged as horror. To use another phrase of Terry Pratchett's, the worm is now on the other boot: 'dark fantasy' is today considered a more respectable and marketable category than 'horror'.

Kirby remembers first being lured towards SF by an issue of a boys' paper called *Modern World* which had a story about a valley of giant insects created by some sinister experiment. Flash Gordon and Buck Rogers were popular childhood attractions at Saturday morning cinema shows.

Facing page:
Deathtrap Equalizer (Corgi 1986) – cover for a 'Tunnels and Trolls' fantasy game tie-in novel by Ken St Andre. This Balrog-like monster exemplifies the old Fantasyland proverb 'Forewarned is four-armed'.

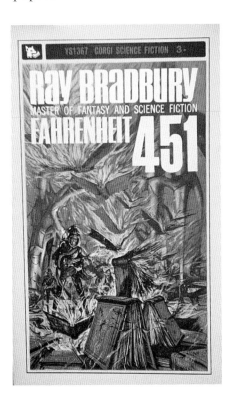

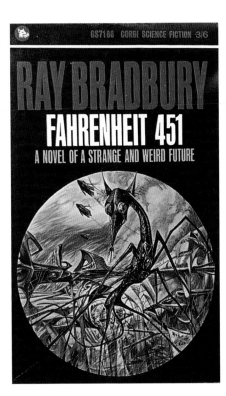

Far left:
Fahrenheit 451 (1953; this cover Corgi 1963) by Ray Bradbury. Montag the fire-man disposes of a small, illicit library in a blaze that shimmers with wrongness. As every SF reader knows, Fahrenheit 451 is supposed to be the temperature at which book-paper ignites and burns. In fact Bradbury plucked this figure from the air: real book-papers begin to burn at a variety of temperatures, all higher than 451°F.

Left:
Fahrenheit 451 II (reissued by Corgi 1965). In this dystopian future, the dread Mechanical Hound hunts down and (with its needle snout) anaesthesizes evil-doers who hoard forbidden contraband – that is, books.

Right:
Cover for 1963 Corgi
edition of Ray Bradbury's
The Silver Locusts, alias *The
Martian Chronicles* (1950).
Kirby was delighted with his
early-60s commissions to
paint covers for all Corgi's
Bradbury paperbacks: at the
time, Bradbury was his
favourite author.

Far right:
Our artist had a second bite
at the apple with *The Silver
Locusts*, probably because
the 1963 painting didn't
adapt well to the new
circular artwork format . . .
so this 1965 Corgi reprint
has a fresh cover whose
spaceship-assaulted disc of
Mars is widely regarded as
a classic SF image.

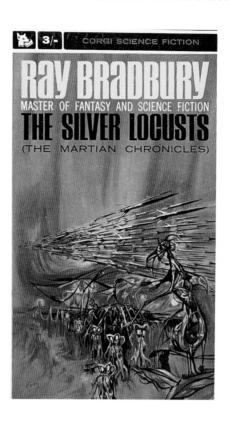

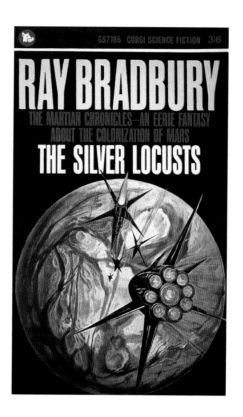

Addiction then took the traditional course, as he sought out the novels of
H.G. Wells and Jules Verne, and went on to make the wonderful discovery
that contemporary SF authors existed.

He still loves the baroque excesses of 'Golden Age' SF's visual imagery,
as formed by the pulps: 'Apart from folklore, the early pulp magazines in
the USA set the conventions. Scantily clad females being menaced and "ten-
tacled" by alien creatures. Impossibly muscled heroes, living brains in glass
cases, robots and spacecraft, all pioneered by the work of artists like Frank
R. Paul. I don't think I created anything, just continued in my own way
what had gone before.'

With the possible exception of living brains in glass cases, Kirby has
been happy to regale us with all these SF images in unstinting crateloads,
sometimes with his tongue detectably in his cheek. If he painted a living
brain in a glass case, it would be recognizably a *Kirby* container of strangely veined glass in subtle curves – as witness his closest approach to this
scene, the cover for Edgar Rice Burroughs's science-fantasy *John Carter of
Mars*, featuring a duel in the monstrous brain-case or helmet of a cyborg
giant (see page 77).

Kirby's idiosyncratic glassware seems to descend in part from one of the
specifically SF artists he most admires: Richard Powers. (Others are Edd
Cartier, Jack Gaughan and Emsh – Ed Emshwiller.) As mentioned in the
Magic (Un)Realism chapter, Powers had an idiosyncratic line in semi-
abstract SF imagery, rippling with mysterious energy exchanges, which our
artist found fascinating. Early Kirby SF covers often featured unexplained
networks of spatial discontinuity or lines of force in the sky. In his current
fantasy landscapes, these are echoed as artful traceries of cloud or smoke; in
his SF paintings they tend to become glass visors or domes of force, seamed
and creatively distorted like something hand-blown by the Alchemists'
Guild of Discworld.

There is a flavour of Powers in the stylized background and almost abstract golden Martians in Kirby's first cover for the SF classic *The Silver Locusts* – also known as *The Martian Chronicles* – by Ray Bradbury. Powers's odd organometallic forms are perhaps remembered in the Mechanical Hound which dominates the second, circular Kirby design for *Fahrenheit 451*. An example of the characteristic early-Kirby traceries of force can be seen in the background of his cover for *The Illustrated Man*.

The hellish patterns of flame from blazing books in the first *Fahrenheit 451* painting are obviously related to such lines of energy. For book-lovers, Bradbury's dystopia where books are proscribed and burnt is peculiarly horrible; yet the satirical rhetoric of *Fahrenheit 451* weirdly anticipates modern excesses of 'political correctness': 'Coloured people don't like

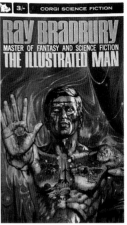

Above:
Ray Bradbury's *The Illustrated Man* (1951; this Corgi cover 1963) – Kirby is proud to say that the original of this was acquired by Bradbury for his private collection. The 1965 Corgi reprint used a circular detail from the painting, showing slightly more of the Illustrated Man's left arm.

Left:
'When I grow up I want to be the Mekon . . .' Illustrating *A Darkness in My Soul* (1972; this cover undated 1976 reprint of 1974 DAW edition) by Dean R. Koontz, who wrote a number of somewhat pot-boiling SF novels like this one before building a new career as a bestselling author of horror, suspense and even (though no longer labelled as such) further SF.

73

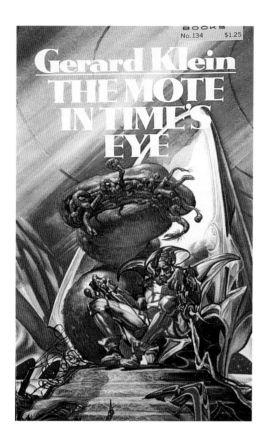

Above left:
A rather jolly monster adorns this cover for Gerard Klein's *The Mote in Time's Eye* (1965 in French as *Les tueurs du temps*; translation DAW 1975). One wonders whether the seated chap is waiting for an excitable audience to shout 'LOOK BEHIND YOU!'

Above right:
Diplomat der Sterne (Diplomat to the Stars; Terra SF, date uncertain) – a German-translated collection of Keith Laumer's comic SF stories about Earth's interstellar diplomat Retief, who finds odd-shaped and nefarious aliens easier to deal with than his own bumbling superiors. The original of this painting – not in fact based on Laumer's book – is in the collection of Forrest J. Ackerman.

Little Black Sambo. Burn it. White people don't feel good about *Uncle Tom's Cabin*. Burn it. Someone's written a book about tobacco and cancer of the lungs? The cigarette people are weeping? Burn the book.'

Kirby has uncompromising feelings in this area. '"Politically Correct" refers to the attempt of certain groups to restrict the freedom to use some words, expressions, and/or images they feel might cause offence or discomfort. It has resulted in diminished variety and richness of language, and impeded creativity as all such suppression must. Over the centuries many attempts have been made to shackle the imagination. Let's hope this latest one does not succeed. The Fantasy world would die if the imagination could not roam free.'

Bradbury himself echoes this last sentiment in a story called 'Usher II' contained in *The Silver Locusts*, which rages against the eager censors who want to 'protect' children from fairytales and fantasy and indeed anything at all that isn't sternly, earnestly real.

Many SF fans and collectors regard these Bradbury covers by Kirby as the definitive, unforgettable accompaniments to the books. Ray Bradbury himself was delighted to acquire the original paintings for *Something Wicked This Way Comes* (not included here) and *The Illustrated Man*. The latter is a marvellous evocation of the framing device of the book, an encounter with this man whose very special tattoos – when viewed by night – glow and move and enact the 18 stories of Bradbury's collection.

Sadly, a fair amount of Kirby's early paperback work isn't acknowledged by the artist, even though collectors of British 1950s and 1960s paperbacks think very highly of these cover illustrations. His love of the fantastic made him unhappy with work that allowed no personal stylistic flourish, including actual SF covers whose science-fictional aspects had had to be 'watered down' on the instructions of art editors. Why did they do this? In the 1950s especially, the SF market was very small. . .

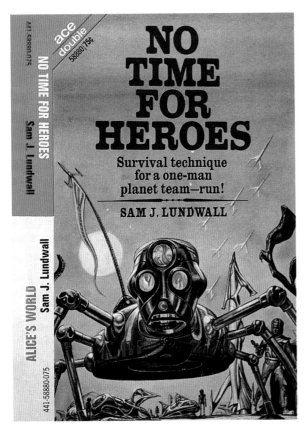

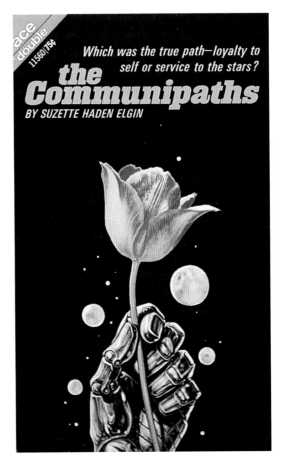

Above left:
This slightly pathetic-looking spider-robot illustrated *No Time for Heroes* (Ace 1970) by Sam J. Lundwall – although, having six rather than eight legs, it's more of a beetle form than a spider.

Above:
A simple but powerful symbolic piece for *The Communipaths* (1970 Ace) by Suzette Haden Elgin, one of Elgin's tales of galactic super-telepath Coyote Jones.

Left:
Not shown in this picture for *Aldair: Master of Ships* (DAW 1977) by Neal Barrett, Jr is series hero Aldair himself, who happened to be a pig genetically modified into humanoid form. We all know someone or other of whom this might be suspected.

Below:
A lonely planetary landscape illustrates *Planet of Exile* (1966; this cover Ace 1970) by Ursula K. Le Guin . . . a very early novel by an author who became one of our most highly regarded creators of SF and fantasy.

Above:
The Best of Kuttner 2 (1965; this cover Mayflower 1970), second volume of a fat anthology of Henry Kuttner's SF and fantasy. The painting illustrates 'The Proud Robot', whose title character Joe irritatingly ignores his creator's orders and prefers to admire the ineffable beauty of his own internal mechanisms, taste-fully laid bare by his 'transplastic' casing.

Above right:
La geste de Kadji – French edition of Lin Carter's fantasy *The Quest of Kadji* (1971). Kirby suspects that he originally painted this for one of Edgar Rice Burroughs's science fantasies about John Carter of Mars, probably *A Fighting Man of Mars* (1931).

'"Watered down" refers to the publishing wish to make the cover look as if it could be an adventure story – a little ambiguous, to catch two markets. My first *Authentic SF* cover was simply a girl running from a fight scene. The publisher projected an attitude of mind that gave a feel of constriction . . . not to step too much out of line.'

Steve Holland, author of that useful study *The Mushroom Jungle: A History of Postwar Paperback Publishing* (1993), has compiled a list of over 40 non-SF Kirby covers from Panther Books alone in the period 1955-60 – none of them included in Kirby's own catalogue of his book cover work, which admits to just nine Panthers in that era. Holland particularly admires our artist's versatility – crime, nonfiction, war, westerns, and more – and declares that one can tell Panther thought highly of him since he was commissioned for several movie tie-in editions, a job reserved for the best artists in a publisher's stable. Out of deference to Kirby's own feelings, none of these 'lost' covers appear here.

'I needed the income so I conformed, rendering these paintings of no value for my collection. I stopped when I could.'

Besides watered-down art there is watered-down science fiction like that of John Lymington, who tended to use tepid SF rationales as a basis for low-key horror novels in which Nasty Things (often merely glimpsed or kept altogether offstage) would menace rustic British communities. Kirby's cover for *The Coming of the Strangers* added considerable pep to a dullish book, with its horde of insectile-crustacean alien uglies whose multi-legged creepiness recalls the Mechanical Hound.

Such weird aliens in Kirby's SF paintings have been much admired; the 1979 *Encyclopedia of Science Fiction*, ed. Peter Nicholls, remarks that 'His

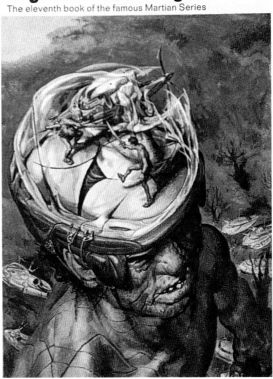

aliens are probably the most grotesquely conceived in SF illustration today.' (The vanishing of this sentence from the 1993 second edition, ed. John Clute and Peter Nicholls, indicates how – in the wake of Discworld – Kirby is now mainly thought of as a comic-fantasy artist.) Further grotesques appear in several covers featured here.

The surly little being painted for *A Darkness in My Soul* by Dean R. Koontz is not an actual extraterrestrial but an evil and prematurely aged mutant child with vast mental powers (quite a common phenomenon in SF – one imagines such stories being written by harassed new parents during sleepless nights). Its childlike size is emphasized not only by an enlarged head but by the exaggerated back and sides of that flamboyant chair or throne. A far less anthropomorphic beastie whiffles and burbles while waving a variety of sensors and appendages in the cover for Gerard Klein's *The Mote in Time's Eye*. Of the painting eventually used in Germany on Keith Laumer's *Diplomat der Sterne*, Kirby remembers only that this planetary landfall scene with its odd aliens was done speculatively 'as an off-shoot of a cover I did for *Authentic*, but years later'.

The *Diplomat der Sterne* spaceship is another bulgy, asymmetrical, organic-metallic form – slightly reminiscent, once again, of Richard Powers's. A background group of towers in similar style is the most immediately and recognizably Kirbyesque element in his painting for Neal Barrett Jr's *Aldair, Master of Ships*, and a single, particularly knobbed and convoluted specimen dominates the cover of *Planet of Exile* by Ursula K. Le Guin.

Organic-seeming curves also take on the glitter of steel in Kirby's various robot creations. For Sam J. Lundwall's *No Time for Heroes* he came up with a spiderlike mechanism whose 'face' or sensor-cluster suggests a

Above left:
Prince of Scorpio (1974; this cover DAW 1976 reprint), from Alan Burt Akers's long-running series about mighty-thewed hero Dray Prescot . . . one of the more enjoyable literary offspring of Burroughs's John Carter of Mars. Alan Burt Akers is a pseudonym of Kenneth Bulmer.

Above right:
John Carter of Mars (1964; this cover Four Square 1967) by Edgar Rice Burroughs. In the included story 'John Carter and the Giant of Mars', Carter does indeed indulge in swordplay, get confined by glass barriers, and have trouble with a 130-foot synthetic giant called Joog. Kirby's imagination combines these elements into a memorable scene not actually found in the text.

FOUR SQUARE SCIENCE-FICTION 3/6

Escape on Venus:
Edgar Rice Burroughs
A world of weird people and uncanny kingdoms

Above:
Escape on Venus (1946; this cover Four Square 1966) by Edgar Rice Burroughs. Luscious Duare, Princess of Vepaja, is not only good in a fight but has a body considered fanciable even by the book's 'human amoebae' – whose hot desire is presumably to hug her tight and ecstatically split in two.

Facing page:
Although Fritz Leiber's *The Swords of Lankhmar* (1968; this cover Mayflower 1970) is pure sword-and-sorcery fantasy, it does indeed contain this 'space-man' visitor from somewhere called Tomorrow, a voluble German who is collecting monsters for the *Zeitgarten* or Time Zoo.

certain curious sadness. A more conventional SF robot compromise between humanoid form and mechanical jointing stands nonplussed on the cover for *Alice's World*, also by Lundwall.

Suzette Haden Elgin's *The Communipaths* is one of a series turning on interstellar communication difficulties which continue despite the existence of telepathy. Here Kirby's treatment is indirect and metaphorical, suggesting the kind of fundamental communication problem that troubles artificial-intelligence workers: could a robot ever appreciate the beauty of a flower? Conversely, the illustration for *The Best of Kuttner 2* seems at first glance to be symbolic – we see right through the outer skin of a 'Visible Man' figure to the strange shapes within – but is actually quite true to Henry Kuttner's description of a comically vain robot in one included story. This was originally painted with a black background, and appeared thus but mirror-reversed on *The Best of Kuttner 1*.

Science fiction and fantasy intersect in the heady hybrid subgenre called science fantasy, where swords meet ray-guns, heroes flex their mighty thews for the benefit of voluptuous ladies, and the only good alien is generally a dead one. 'The barbaric ornamentation and the motley crew of plug-uglies, not forgetting assorted un-earthly monsters to contest with, give a world richly in contradiction with the grey drab of the workaday world, and such rich ground for the illustrator to have fun with. . .'

In this vein, the atypically unmuscular hero figure in the painting for *La geste de Kadji* by Lin Carter is ready for battle on three fronts, equipped as he is with sword, blaster and posing pouch. This subgenre's invariably busty women have the option of either sprawling on a throne to be admired by the exotic throng, as in the cover for Alan Burt Akers's *Prince of Scorpio*, or grabbing a death-ray and plunging into the fray like the feistier Duare, Princess of Vepaja, in *Escape on Venus* by Edgar Rice Burroughs.

Such splendid women are archetypal images of fantasy and science fantasy, and Kirby feels strongly about the importance of archetypes. He's sometimes been asked just why the nondescript or demurely dressed females in Terry Pratchett's stories tend to blossom in his cover paintings into Duare, Princess of Vepaja, or some close approximation. His determined answer: 'It's the same way the heroes are exaggerated. Demure dress is not appropriate to SF/fantasy . . . exaggeration is the name of the game. That, combined with established SF/fantasy convention.'

Serious pure-fantasy covers, played dead straight, are relatively rare in this artist's output. A few examples are the looming multi-armed monster painted for Ken St Andre's *Deathtrap Equalizer*; the bloody-sworded knight who has just slain a dragon on the cover of Lin Carter's *The Year's Best Fantasy Stories: 3*; and a gaudily dressed 'spaceman' riding a sea-serpent just as described in Fritz Leiber's wittiest fantasy novel, *The Swords of Lankhmar*. The last cover's visored suit was probably useful SF-like protective coloration in those bygone days of 1970, before the British fantasy genre market had taken off.

For William Rotsler's novel *Patron of the Arts*, Kirby seized on the parts of the book set on Mars and dealing with an enigmatic artefact which is

Top:
The pattern of buildings on this cover for *Alice's World* (Ace 1970) by Sam J. Lundwall gently suggests the chessboard landscape in Lewis Carroll's *Through the Looking-Glass*.

Above:
A leggy alien horde painted for *The Coming of the Strangers* (1961; this cover Corgi 1963) by John Lymington, author of generally mediocre SF/horror novels. Lymington was more successful with mediocre detective fiction written under his real name John Newton Chance.

Above:
Patron of the Arts (1974; this cover Elmfield 1975) by William Rotsler – whose central
SF device, a new art form, was almost by definition impossible to draw. Instead, the
setting for parts of the story suggested this roseate Martian landscape, which preceded
the Viking landers' confirmation of how dark the sky actually appears on Mars.

The Year's Best Fantasy Stories III (DAW 1977) edited by Lin Carter. According to the colour-coded taxonomy of Diana Wynne Jones's invaluable The Tough Guide to Fantasyland (1996) the knight shown here is very probably evil, since he seems to have the infallible indicator of glowing red eyes.

UW1338

DAW sf
BOOKS
No. 267 $1.50

LIN CARTER
PRESENTS
THE YEAR'S BEST
FANTASY
STORIES: 3

both a work of art and a galactic computer. The red desolation of Mars is painted with sweeping simplicity, with a domed human colony in the distance and a clump of spiky red artefacts which certainly are enigmatic.

The SF paintings discussed in this chapter seem very different from Kirby's main present-day output. Perhaps surprisingly, he considers this change a matter of content rather than something resulting from any evolution of his personal style: 'My style remains much the same, modified by the subject matter, humorous fantasy needing a different feel from serious fantasy/SF. Any efforts to improve are towards technical excellence and finding a more "astonishing" way of painting things.' Like so many accomplished artists, he is never quite satisfied with his work.

CHAPTER SIX

DISCWORLD REVISITED

This book's first chapter, Discworld Delights, explored a variety of Discworld paintings used on the covers of Terry Pratchett's books; but that's only part of the story. Discworld has become a vast and slightly terrifying publishing phenomenon, with many spinoffs: a music CD, diaries, cassette readings, graphic novels, figurines, t-shirts, playscripts, maps, posters, computer games, jigsaws, candles, keyrings, postcards, fine-art prints, embroidery kits, ornamental plates, greetings cards, jewellery, mouse mats, and so on forever.

Josh Kirby is always glad of the chance to spread himself in formats other than book covers. He clearly had particular fun with his *Rincewind and the Luggage* poster for Isis and the paintings titled *Ankh-Morpork*, *Unseen University* and *When Will We Three Meet Again?* which accompanied the *From the Discworld* music CD.

Also less constrained than book covers are the paintings done for CD-ROM computer-game boxes. There have been four Discworld computer games, all in the puzzle-solving 'Adventure' mould rather than shoot-'em-up action. Kirby's illustrations for the most recent three appear

Overleaf:
Ankh-Morpork. . .
the greatest, sleaziest and smelliest city of the Discworld, impressionist-ically painted for Dave Greenslade's CD music album *From the Discworld* (Virgin 1994).

Rincewind and the Luggage – a 1995 painting issued by Isis as an undated 17¼ in x 25 in (45 cm x 64 cm) poster, limited to 2000 numbered copies signed by the artist. Characters from several different Discworld novels are assembled for this elabo-rate scene that never was.

Unseen University – Terry Pratchett's logical successor to the Invisible College of real-world history, in another illustration for Dave Greenslade's music album *From the Discworld* (Virgin 1994).

here: the titles are *Discworld* (here *Discworld III*), *Missing, Presumed . . .!?* (whose painting Kirby thinks of as *Rincewind and Binky*), and *Discworld Noir*. A much earlier and clunkier game, *The Colour of Magic*, ran only on the Amstrad CPC, Commodore 64 and Spectrum, and is fondly remembered by fans.

Some of the teeming spinoffs gave Kirby no pleasure. In 1995 Gollancz came up with the idea of 'Compact Discworld' editions, tiny versions of the first four Discworld novels that were printed in China with pages less than 3 $1/2$ in (9 cm) high. The type was unexpectedly legible, but rather than commission new Kirby covers that would work at this size, the publishers extracted details from his existing paintings and plonked them down on a white background. It still rankles:

'The mini book covers were awful, I think, and demonstrated the lack of understanding, in the Gollancz art department or management, of Terry Pratchett's work; not to mention their disregard of my artwork and the fact that fans like to see my paintings in connection with Terry's books and need not be pushed aside like an idiot son.'

Other regular annoyances include mirror-reversals of pictures whose whole design is based on the Kirby patent spiral – see Magic (Un)Realism – and Western readers' left-to-right scanning of a picture. Sometimes, of course, there's a logical reason for this change: 'On Hebrew editions they start from the back! Also Japanese editions.'

The most bizarre mismatches of picture and book were reliably perpetrated by Heyne in Germany, whose design department works in a

Left:
When Will We Three Meet Again? The smallest coven of witches in fiction assembles on a suitably blasted heath . . . painted for Dave Greenslade's music album *From the Discworld* (Virgin 1994) and later re-used on the Terry Pratchett omnibus volume *The Witches Trilogy* (Gollancz 1994).

Below:
Discworld III – cover for the first Discworld computer game for PC, Macintosh and Playstation machines. The title was simply *Discworld* (Perfect Entertainment/Psygnosis, 1995). Another view of Discworld as a whole, with Death and the perpetually terrified Rincewind zooming through space on the Luggage. The game-player 'controls' Rincewind, who needs to solve the problem of a dragon – from *Guards! Guards!* – which is terrorizing Ankh-Morpork city.

separate building and, as Colin Smythe wrote in a 1998 article on 15 years of covers inflicted on *The Colour of Magic*, is 'considered even by Heyne staff to be a law unto itself'. Thus the first German edition of *The Colour of Magic* (inexplicably bound with the fifth Discworld book, *Sourcery*) boasted a Kirby jacket belonging to one of Robert Rankin's 'Brentford' titles, *The Sprouts of Wrath*. Although Pratchett contracts include a penalty clause that can be invoked if unsuitable artwork is used, Heyne refused to accept that a picture featuring a Morris Minor, a pub, a gasometer and London policemen was in any way inappropriate to Discworld.

Another Heyne translation, that of *Equal Rites* (*Das Erbe des Zauberers* or 'The Wizard's Heir' – the title pun wouldn't work in German), annoyed both Kirby and Pratchett with a cover that used a detail from one of the Ayeguy paintings, *Arrival of the Ark*. As Pratchett has remarked, 'Heyne in particular were good at picking covers at random out of a big sack.' One of his comic SF novels was released with a crucifixion scene on the jacket. . .

While Kirby's vision of Discworld is widely thought definitive, it follows from human nature that this feeling is not quite universal. As a general rule no artist's impression can hope to match every reader's.

Rincewind and Binky – painted for the packaging of the second Discworld computer game produced for PC/Mac/Playstation systems: *Missing, Presumed . . . !?* (Perfect Entertainment/Psygnosis, 1997). As in *Reaper Man*, the missing person is Death; his absence and its side-effects lead to a succession of puzzles for Rincewind. No one knows why Death felt the only possible name for his awesome pale horse was Binky.

Discworld Noir, Kirby's painting for the latest Discworld computer game (Perfect Entertainment/GT Interactive, 1999). A trenchcoated ex-Watchman P.I. in the mean streets of Ankh-Morpork is confronted with grim criminal challenges, much darker in tone than those of previous games. Very Discworld, very *noir*.

Although Kirby agrees that 'the continuing attempt is to strive to get it "just so",' he defines this as 'trying to reproduce exactly what is in my mind, a goal never quite reached'. There are those who insist politely but firmly that Kirby is painting an alternate and very nice-looking Discworld that happens not to be the real one in *their* mind's eye. Which is only fair, since Pratchett explains away his own occasional inconsistencies by insisting that although there is only one Discworld, it has alternative and perhaps mutually exclusive pasts.

One specific point that has bothered the fans, and also to some small extent the author himself, is that on her first appearance – on the cover of *Equal Rites* – the unforgettable witch Granny Weatherwax looks like a hag, with a monstrous hook-nose *and warts.*

With Granny, in fact, Pratchett clearly meant to ring a few changes on the stereotype of a witch (though her debut in *Equal Rites* doesn't really show her later stature). She is the indomitable old lady that every family knows or remembers, whose total, pigheaded belief in her rightness makes her unchallengeable even when in the wrong. Unfortunately it's only rather late in that first Weatherwax book that we learn that 'Granny suffered from robustly healthy teeth' and rather envies a colleague – Nanny Annaple – who's lost all hers and so has 'real crone-credibility'. Similarly:

'And then there was warts. Without any effort Nanny managed to get a face like a sockful of marbles, while Granny had tried every reputable wart-causer and failed to raise even the obligatory nose wart. Some witches had all the luck.'

Of course Kirby has the perfect reply to hand in the text of various later Discworld stories. Discworld, which Pratchett has repeatedly called a 'world and mirror of worlds', is dominated by expectations, by the power and momentum of Story: 'narrative causality'. Even indomitable Granny has great difficulty in derailing rogue stories whose narrative impetus is

Overleaf, left:
The Sea and Little Fishes I (Discworld Convention Programme Book 1998), illustrating a scene which Terry Pratchett had removed from the story during rewriting. A Pratchett footnote: 'Elements of that scene, somewhat changed, ended up in the "gnarly ground" scene in *Carpe Jugulum*.'

Overleaf, right
The Sea and Little Fishes II, the second and final cover illustration for Terry Pratchett's story in *Legends* ed. Robert Silverberg (HarperCollins Voyager 1998). Granny Weatherwax's cottage furniture includes a hatmaking mould specially designed for constructing a witch's essential Pointy Hat.

Above:
Eric I: Rincewind Running.
All the *Eric* illustrations are
from *Eric: A Discworld
Story* (Gollancz 1990), the
sole Terry Pratchett book
where Kirby gets equal
cover credit and a share of
royalties. Here we meet
Rincewind – the wizzard
who can't even spell 'wizard'
– in a relatively calm and
tranquil moment.

taking them to unacceptable endings. What's more, morphic resonance – a
sort of pseudoscientific rationalization of sympathetic magic in which
effects resemble causes, and things which have happened once are likelier to
happen again – is a basic principle of Discworld physics. So if the image of
Granny Weatherwax is shaped not only by his words but by Kirby's
instinctive understanding of what we all *know* witches look like, Pratchett
has only himself to blame.

Just as he later revised his early conception of the four-eyed Twoflower,
Kirby was able to rethink Granny Weatherwax and extend his range of
witchy figures when she returned in *Wyrd Sisters* – accompanied by
coven-members Nanny Ogg (a multiply-married reprobate looking
cheerfully back on many decades of enthusiastic indiscretion) and Magrat
Garlick (a young and wettish New Age witch with intractably bad hair
made worse by wearing flowers in it). As though giving Nanny Ogg a
decent ration of warts had satisfied some primal artistic need, Kirby allowed
Granny to be wart-free this time around . . . although incipient wartiness
and haggishness keep hovering over his images of her, as seen in *When Shall
We Three Meet Again?*

Kirby defiantly concludes: 'Witches and wizards have their place in far
more ancient folklore and I follow that convention – a sort of communal
consciousness.'

He recently painted Granny Weatherwax twice for Robert Silverberg's
original anthology *Legends*, whose gimmick was to present new stories set
in internationally famous fantasy worlds. Terry Pratchett's contribution,
'The Sea and Little Fishes', inspired two Kirby covers featuring Discworld
witches. The first, showing witchy mayhem in a cave, had to be dropped
when Pratchett agreed to Silverberg's editorial suggestion that the relevant

scene in his story should be removed for length reasons. Pratchett: 'We didn't know that what got sent to Josh was the *pre-edited* text – and, sure enough, he chose to illustrate the scene which had been cut. An everyday adventure in the wonderful world that is Publishing.'

As a result, the 1998 British Discworld convention was able to feature this rare unpublished cover on the front of its souvenir programme book. The new painting shows a deputation of witches headed by Nanny Ogg bursting in on a characteristically bad-tempered Granny Weatherwax – no warts, but bags of personality crackling from her face and pose.

A special and so far unique Discworld project is Terry Pratchett's and Josh Kirby's *Eric* – whose title on the cover is 'Faust' in black-letter Gothic, crossed out and replaced with a scrawled 'Eric'. This was designed from the outset as a collaboration, with Pratchett writing a storyline that deliberately whizzed wildly around in time and space, providing Kirby with opportunities for lavish illustration of the Discworld equivalents of the Big Bang, the sea where life first emerges (from a cheese sandwich abandoned by Rincewind), the bloodthirsty and jungle-dwelling Aztec Empire, the Trojan War, and Hell.

Since all the illustrations were dropped from the 1991 paperback edition of *Eric* (even the cover was replaced with a new painting), Kirby's favourites from this joint effort are reprinted here. *Rincewind Running*, a rare close-up of the world's least talented wizard in his usual state of panic-stricken flight, appeared on the title page. *Eric*'s story begins when spotty young demonologist Eric tries to summon infernal powers to do his bidding, and gets Rincewind instead. The Luggage soon follows, and Rincewind and Eric find themselves flashing through time and space . . . beginning with an aerial view of all Discworld in *Discworld I*.

Overleaf:
Eric IV: Discworld I. The roughly quarter-circle-shaped area at the left is empty and overprinted with text in the original book. Kirby later added further background to complete the painting: 'I sort of designed it with that in mind, but gave up with the rest of the Eric pictures, so they remain as in the book'

Eric VII: Splash Down . . . into the Inca-like Tezuman Empire. Jungle denizens include a lurid tree frog and a snake whose natural shape is just such a serpentine line as Kirby loves to draw. The book version has some text in the white space at the right.

Above:
Eric VIII: Triumphal Procession. Since this is South America, Discworld style, there are naturally llamas. Young Eric has been hoping for 'mysterious ancient races of Amazonian princesses who subject all male prisoners to strange and exhausting progenitative rites'. Needless to say, he doesn't find any, but Kirby slips in a voluptuously atypical Tezuwoman at far right anyway.

Opposite above:
Eric X: The Tsortean Horse. This wooden horse's lovingly portrayed outrage really needs no comment. Its builder, wrote Pratchett, 'could have put the exit hatch in a more dignified place, but for humorous reasons had apparently decided not to'.

Opposite below:
Eric XIII: Primal Sea. Alone, alone, all, all alone. . . Little do Rincewind and Eric know that the evolution of Discworld life will be kick-started by the nutrients in a not very nice cheese sandwich discarded by the wizard on this prehistoric beach.

This soon leads to the *Splash Down* scene, with Eric, Rincewind and the Luggage finding themselves dumped into the jungles of the Tezuman (Aztec) Empire. The murderous Tezumen welcome their visitors suitably in *Triumphal Procession*, which unfortunately is the preliminary to plans for ritual killing. But *Sacrifice* shows this dark deed being interrupted at the last minute by the one Discworld entity more psychopathic than a Tezuman High Priest, the Luggage. The action shifts through time to the equivalent of the Trojan War (between the lands of Ephebe and Tsort), where Rincewind and Eric find themselves inside the huge wooden bulk of the cunning strategem that dominates Kirby's picture *The Tsortean Horse.*. .

Having complicated the outcome of the war, they timeslip to *The Big Bang* and the beginning of creation, and after a brief encounter with the Creator are stranded for a while in an empty Discworld on the ocean shore shown in *Primal Sea*. Eric the demonology hacker manages to transport them to the present day by reversing the operation of a magic summoning circle: 'You rewrite the source codex . . .' This proves to be a leap from a metaphorical frying pan into a literal fire, since the next stop is Hell. In fact demons have been orchestrating all these magical transitions as part of a genuinely diabolical plot. Kirby's final painting, *Mephisto's Party*, depicts the uproarious and balloon-infested infernal celebration as this scheme culminates with Astfgl, the overly officious King of Hell who has introduced new terrors like modern management techniques, being kicked upstairs to become Supreme Life President.

Kirby has also been able to indulge his fondness for illustrating Discworld when painting jacket pictures for further collections which include Discworld stories or characters. His cover art for Peter Haining's comic-fantasy anthologies *The Wizards of Odd* and *The Flying Sorcerers* relates to the Pratchett stories featured in each book. The very short

Eric XV: Mephisto's Party. High jinks in the infernal regions as the King of Hell is given a determinedly jolly send-off party. The picture's private title indicates that Kirby really couldn't cope with the actual name given by Pratchett to this lordly demon: Astfgl. A magic mirror shows Eric and Rincewind furtively escaping up the long stairway (paved of course with good intentions) that runs between Discworld's surface and Hell.

'Theatre of Cruelty' in the first collection inspired a close-up view of the hunky Ankh-Morpork city guardsman Captain Carrot – originally painted to go with this story in a W. H. Smith giveaway magazine – interrogating the troupe of gnomes who have been forced to enact the very cruel tale of Punch and Judy (see pages 106–107).

For the non-Discworld 'Turntables of the Night' in the second Haining book, Kirby seized on its appearance of Death at a real-world disco and gleefully painted the ever-popular, skeletal figure of Discworld's Death in marvellously inappropriate – or appropriate? – disco garb, including massive platform soles and flares. (Pratchett's Death has the same presence and speaks in the same HOLLOW, LEADEN VOICE when encountered on Earth, as also occurs in *Good Omens*.)

A spinoff volume to which Terry Pratchett himself contributed extensively is his and Stephen Briggs's *The Discworld Companion*, a sort of encyclopedia of Discworld. Though compiled and illustrated by Briggs, this incorporates all sorts of Pratchettian oddments which extend our knowledge of institutions like Unseen University and often prefigure parts of Discworld books then yet to be written. (Serious researchers need to remind themselves that this is intended as entertainment, something to browse in rather than a true reference book: trying to look up, say, Rincewind's birth sign, the Small Boring Group of Faint Stars leads to a fruitless search for Astrology, Astronomy, Constellations and Stars, before one finds the information listed only under Zodiac.)

Kirby's cover scene is set, perhaps inevitably, in the Library of Unseen University. Besides the celebrated Librarian, various other Discworld images are lovingly woven in: a witch's hat and broomstick, a wizard's hat and robe, swamp dragons, the Death of Rats and a hanging model of Discworld itself.

One of the least Kirby-like compositions to be found on a Discworld spinoff is the cover for *The Unseen University Challenge*, a quizbook which by staggering coincidence was compiled by the author of the text you are reading. No spirals, no overall sweeping lines of action, just eight familiar Discworld characters in two rows (on the cover) or a single row (in the original painting).

The story here is that, given the idea of a panel of Discworld personalities being subjected to a University Challenge-style quiz, Kirby instantly imagined it 'designed as a spoof of Leonardo's Last Supper – but Gollancz wouldn't have it, so the characters were spaced out to be put in two rows. I painted it in a line partly as a regretful remnant of the thwarted Last Supper idea and partly to have a painting to show at the end. I have a policy not to do a Discworld cover that does not have a framable painting at the end of it, and I suppose I failed on this occasion. I knew they would chop it up on the cover.'

Despite the sheer number of Discworld pictures that he has now painted, Kirby looks forward to doing more. He makes it very clear that he loves the Terry Pratchett books and finds them far from lightweight: 'His social comment is penetrating and exposes human fallibility and frailty in a droll yet relentless light. Not to mention showing the absurdity of social institutions and behaviour.'

All the same, as Tom Holt reminds us in his introduction and this wide-ranging selection has tried to illustrate, Josh Kirby's artistic output is far larger and more varied than many Discworld fans realize. He has created many other images that will endure. Long may he continue.

Theatre of Cruelty – this unusual squashed-down composition was designed for a spread in W. H. Smith's giveaway magazine *Bookcase* (1993), so that Terry Pratchett's very short story could be printed over the empty blue sky. It became the cover for the collection *The Wizards of Odd* (1996) ed. Peter Haining, which uses an expanded version of the same story.

Eric XII: The Big Bang.
When the Discworld
universe first explodes into
being from the void, Death
is already there waiting –
as Rincewind finds when he
blunders into the beginning
of everything. In the book,
this fine composition was
allowed a double-page
spread with no distracting
printed text.

The Discworld Companion (Gollancz 1994, revised Vista 1997). For this 'Definitive and Only Guide' Kirby centred his painting on Unseen University's orang-utan Librarian, admired by many real librarians as a macho role-model whose mere grin can terrify defacers and stealers of books.

BOOK COVERS BY JOSH KIRBY

Dates are from Josh Kirby's records of when he completed or invoiced for each painting. He does not, as a general rule, keep track of foreign-language appearances which were not specific book commissions.

TITLE	DATE	Author	Publisher
Authentic Science Fiction Magazine – 78	1956		
Authentic Science Fiction Magazine – 80	1957		
Authentic Science Fiction Magazine – 81	1957		
Authentic Science Fiction Magazine – 82	1957		
Authentic Science Fiction Magazine – 83	1957		
Authentic Science Fiction Magazine – 84	1957		
Cee-Tee Man	1954	Dan Morgan	Panther
Moonraker	1956	Ian Fleming	Pan Books
Return to Tomorrow	1957	L. Ron Hubbard	Panther
Split Image	1957	Reed R. De Rouen	Panther
Escape to Venus	1958	S. Makepeace Lott	Panther
The Currents of Space	1958	Isaac Asimov	Panther
Revenge of Frankenstein	1958	Jimmy Sangster	Panther
The Caves of Steel	1958	Isaac Asimov	Panther
Seed of Light	1960	Edmund Cooper	Panther
The Twenty-Second Century	1960	John Christopher	Panther
Ossian's Ride	1960	Fred Hoyle	Four Square
Man Drowning	1961	Henry Kuttner	Four Square
The Evil Eye	1961	Pierre Boileau and Thomas Narcejac	Four Square
The 27th Day	1961	John Mantley	Four Square
Ahead of Time	1961	Henry Kuttner	Four Square
Planet of the Dreamers	1961	John D. MacDonald	Corgi
Occam's Razor	1962	David Duncan	Four Square
The Scarlet Boy	1962	Arthur C. Marshall	Corgi
Shock!	1962	Richard Matheson	Corgi
Angels and Spaceships	1962	Fredric Brown	Four Square
The Grey Ones	1962	John Lymington	Corgi
The Coming of the Strangers	1962	John Lymington	Corgi
The Other Side of the Sky	1962	Arthur C. Clarke	Corgi
A Sword Above the Night	1962	John Lymington	Corgi
The Illustrated Man	1963	Ray Bradbury	Corgi
The Silver Locusts	1963	Ray Bradbury	Corgi
Fahrenheit 451	1963	Ray Bradbury	Corgi
Saturn Over the Water	1963	J.B. Priestley	Corgi
The Haunters and the Haunted	1963	(Anthology)	Corgi
Far Out	1963	Damon Knight	Corgi
The Sentinel Stars	1963	Louis Charbonneau	Corgi
Benighted	1963	J.B. Priestley	Corgi
Twisted	1963	Ed. Groff Conklin	Consul
Creeps by Night	1963	Ed. Dashiell Hammett	Consul
The Illustrated Man	1964	Ray Bradbury	Corgi
The Hour of the Phoenix	1964	Richard Saxon	Consul
Half in Shadow	1964	Mary E. Counselman	Consul
Timeliner	1964	Charles Eric Maine	Corgi
The Night Spiders	1964	John Lymington	Corgi
Beyond Infinity	1964	Alan E. Nourse	Corgi
The Dreamers	1964	Roger Manvell	Corgi
Count-Down	1964	Charles Eric Maine	Corgi
Nightmares	1964	?Robert Bloch	Corgi
The Last Leap	1964	Daniel F. Galouye	Corgi
The Sleep Eaters	1964	John Lymington	Corgi
A Stir of Echoes	1964	Richard Matheson	Corgi
Tales of Horror and the Supernatural	1964	Arthur Machen	Panther
Propeller Island	1964	Jules Verne	Panther
The Golden Apples of the Sun	1964	Ray Bradbury	Corgi
Something Wicked this way Comes	1964	Ray Bradbury	Corgi
Fahrenheit 451	1964	Ray Bradbury	Corgi
The Silver Locusts	1964	Ray Bradbury	Corgi
The Dark Mind	1964	Colin Kapp	Corgi
Weird Shadows From Beyond	1965	Ed. John Carnell	Panther
Nelson Algren's Book of Lonely Monsters	1965	Nelson Algren	Panther
The Shores of Space	1965	Richard Matheson	Corgi
Men, Martians and Machines	1965	Eric Frank Russell	Panther
Marooned	1965	Martin Caidin	Corgi
Black Tales	1965	Ed. anonymous	Corgi
The Novel of the Black Seal	1965	Arthur Machen	Corgi
The Novel of the White Powder	1965	Arthur Machen	Corgi
Horror-7	1965	Robert Bloch	Corgi
Shock II	1965	Richard Matheson	Corgi

Journey Beyond Tomorrow	1965	Robert Sheckley	Corgi
Horror Cover II	1965	?	Panther
Haunted Houseful	1965	Ed. Alfred Hitchcock	Four Square
My Bones and My Flute	1965	Edgar Mittelholzer	Corgi
Sundog	1965	Brian Ball	Corgi
The Elixir of Life	1965	Harrison Ainsworth	Four Square
Vathek	1966	William Beckford	Four Square
Melmoth the Wanderer	1966	Charles Maturin	Four Square
Beyond the Curtain of Dark	1966	Ed. Peter Haining	Four Square
A Fighting Man of Mars	1966	Edgar Rice Burroughs	Four Square
The Night Side	1966	Ed. August Derleth	Four Square
The Craft of Terror	1966	Ed. Peter Haining	Four Square
Escape on Venus	1966	Edgar Rice Burroughs	Four Square
Chain Reaction	1966	Christopher Hodder-Williams	Corgi
Swords of Mars	1966	Edgar Rice Burroughs	Four Square
The Lodger	1966	Marie Belloc-Lowndes	Four Square
Shards of Space	1966	Robert Sheckley	Corgi
The Other Side of the Sky	1966	Arthur C. Clarke	Corgi
Llana of Gathol	1966	Edgar Rice Burroughs	Four Square
Carson of Venus	1966	Edgar Rice Burroughs	Four Square
John Carter of Mars	1966	Edgar Rice Burroughs	Four Square
The Weird Ones	1966	Ed. H.L. Gold	Corgi
Behind the Locked Door	1966	Ed. Alfred Hitchcock	Four Square
The New Minds	1966	Dan Morgan	Corgi
Untouched by Human Hands	1966	Robert Sheckley	Four Square
Meet Death at Night	1966	Ed. Alfred Hitchcock	Four Square
I Can't Sleep at Night	1966	Ed. Kurt Singer	Corgi
The Shape of Things to Come	1967	H.G. Wells	Corgi
Tarzan of the Apes	1967	Edgar Rice Burroughs	Four Square
The Interpreter	1967	Brian Aldiss	Four Square
Anyone for Murder?	1967	Ed. Alfred Hitchcock	NEL
The Late Unlamented	1967	Ed. Alfred Hitchcock	NEL
Tarzan and the City of Gold	1967	Edgar Rice Burroughs	NEL
Tarzan and the Madman	1967	Edgar Rice Burroughs	NEL
Tarzan the Magnificent	1967	Edgar Rice Burroughs	NEL
Tarzan at the Earth's Core	1967	Edgar Rice Burroughs	NEL
Tarzan and the Ant Men	1967	Edgar Rice Burroughs	NEL
Tarzan and the Leopard Men	1967	Edgar Rice Burroughs	NEL
Tarzan Jungle Tales	1967	Edgar Rice Burroughs	NEL
Tarzan the Invincible	1967	Edgar Rice Burroughs	NEL
Tarzan's Quest	1967	Edgar Rice Burroughs	NEL
Tarzan and the Castaways	1967	Edgar Rice Burroughs	NEL
Tarzan and the Forbidden City	1967	Edgar Rice Burroughs	NEL
New Writings in SF 11	1967	Ed. John Carnell	Corgi
(cover for Flight of a Plastic Bee by John Rankine)			
Tarzan and the Jewels of Opar	1967	Edgar Rice Burroughs	NEL
Breakdown	1967	Ed. Dashiell Hammett	NEL
The Lost Perception	1967	Daniel F. Galouye	Corgi
The Menace from Earth	1967	Robert A. Heinlein	Corgi
New Writings in SF 12	1968	Ed. John Carnell	Corgi
(Cover for Vertigo by James White)			
Close to Critical	1968	Hal Clement	Corgi
The Graveyard Man	1968	Ed. Alfred Hitchcock	NEL
The Unquiet Grave	1968	Ed. August Derleth	Four Square
The Other Foot	1968	Damon Knight	Corgi
New Writings in SF 13	1968	Ed. John Carnell	Corgi
(Cover for The Divided House by John Rackham)			
Nightshade and Damnations	1968	Gerald Kersh	Hodder/Coronet
The Biological Time Bomb	1969	G Rattray Taylor	Panther
The Chinese Maze Murders	1969	Robert van Gulik	Panther
The Chinese Bell Murders	1969	Robert van Gulik	Panther
The Phantom of the Temple	1969	Robert van Gulik	Panther
New Writings in SF 14	1969	Ed. John Carnell	Corgi
(Cover for The Ballad of Luna Lil by Sydney J. Bounds)			
Necklace and Calabash	1969	Robert van Gulik	Panther
The City and the Stars	1969	Arthur C. Clarke	Corgi
I Sing the Body Electric	1969	Ray Bradbury	Sidgwick & Jackson
A Century of SF Novels	1969	Ed. Damon Knight	Mayflower
Blue Moon	1969	Ed. Douglas Lindsay	Mayflower
A Century of Great Short SF Novels	1969	Ed. Damon Knight	Mayflower

Following pages:
Cover for Peter Haining's anthology *The Flying Sorcerers: More Comic Tales of Fantasy* (1997) –
illustrating the included Pratchett story 'Turntables of the Night'. From Death's conversation at a disco we
discover that he collects the Beatles. But he hasn't got them all yet. . .

The Reproductive System	1969	John Sladek	Mayflower
The Best of Sci-Fi 12	1969	Ed. Judith Merril	Mayflower
SF The Best of the Best Part I	1969	Ed. Judith Merril	Mayflower
SF The Best of the Best Part II	1969	Ed. Judith Merril	Mayflower
Galactic Odyssey	1970	Keith Laumer	Mayflower
Dark Ways to Death	1970	Peter Saxon	Mayflower
Worlds of the Imperium	1970	Keith Laumer	Mayflower
The Dance of the Dwarfs	1970	Geoffrey Household	Mayflower
The Aliens Among Us	1970	James White	Corgi
Gallows on the Sand	1970	Morris West	Mayflower
Dark Mind, Dark Heart	1970	Ed. August Derleth	Mayflower
Satan's Child	1970	Peter Saxon	Mayflower
Undersea Quest	1970	Frederik Pohl and Jack Williamson	Mayflower
Undersea Fleet	1970	Frederik Pohl and Jack Williamson	Mayflower
Undersea City	1970	Frederik Pohl and Jack Williamson	Mayflower
The Best of Kuttner 1	1970	Henry Kuttner	Mayflower
The Best of Kuttner 2	1970	Henry Kuttner	Mayflower
One Against Time	1970	Astron Del Martia	Mayflower
The Plastic Magicians	1970	Peter Leslie	Mayflower
The Communipaths	1970	Suzette Hayden Elgin	Ace
The Gates of Time	1970	Neal Barrett, Jr	Ace
The Stone God Awakens	1970	Philip José Farmer	Ace
The Swords of Lankhmar	1970	Fritz Leiber	Mayflower
Dimension of Miracles	1970	Robert Sheckley	Mayflower
Alice's World	1970	Sam J. Lundwall	Ace
No Time for Heroes	1970	Sam J. Lundwall	Ace
The Monitors	1970	Keith Laumer	Mayflower
The Shark Hunters	1970	W.A. Ballinger (William Howard Baker)	Mayflower
Planet of Exile	1970	Ursula K. Le Guin	Ace
Warlocks and Warriors	1970	Ed. L. Sprague de Camp	Mayflower
The God of the Labyrinth	1971	Colin Wilson	Mayflower
Son of the Tree	1971	Jack Vance	Ace
Bar the Doors	1971	Ed. Alfred Hitchcock	Mayflower
The Secret of the Lost Race	1971	Andre Norton	Ace
The Mind Behind the Eye	1972	Joseph Green	DAW
A Man Called Poe	1972	Sam Moskowitz	Sphere
The Day Before Tomorrow	1972	Gerard Klein	DAW
The Ice People	1972	Rene Barjavel	Mayflower
Ole Doc Methuselah	1972	L. Ron Hubbard	DAW
Ensign Flandry	1972	Pohl Anderson	Lancer
Bumsider	1972	C.C. MacApp	Lancer
A Month of Mystery	1972	Ed. Alfred Hitchcock	Pan
The Witchcraft Reader	1972	Ed. Peter Haining	Pan
The Jagged Orbit	1972	John Brunner	Ace
The Left Hand of Darkness	1972	Ursula K. Le Guin	Ace
Tales of Supernatural Terror	1972	Guy de Maupassant	Pan
Tomorrow Lies in Ambush	1972	Bob Shaw	Ace
Victory on Janus	1972	Andre Norton	Ace
Storm Over Warlock	1972	Andre Norton	Ace
Time Story	1972	Stuart Gordon	DAW
The Elephant Man	1972	Frederick Treaves	Ballantine
Vanity of Duluoz	1972	Jack Kerouac	Quartet
Fireworks	1973	?	Ace
The Case of the Friendly Corpse	1973	L. Ron Hubbard	Ace
What's Become of Screwloose?	1973	Ron Goulart	DAW
The Lord's Pink Ocean	1973	David Walker	DAW
13th Pan Book of Horror Stories	1973	Herbert van Thal	Pan
Book of the Werewolf	1973	Brian J. Frost	Sphere
The Hero of Downways	1973	Michael G. Coney	DAW
The World Menders	1973	Lloyd Biggle, Jr	Morley
Alien Planet	1973	Fletcher Pratt	Ace
Syzygy	1973	Michael G. Coney	DAW
The Town and the City	1973	Jack Kerouac	Quartet
Is There Anybody There?	1973	Norah Lofts	Corgi
Rolling Gravestones	1973	Ed. Alfred Hitchcock	Mayflower
Swampworld West	1973	Perry A. Chapdelaine	Morley
Midsummer Century	1973	James Blish	DAW
Games Killers Play	1973	Ed. Alfred Hitchcock	Mayflower
Alfred Hitchcock's Death Bag	1973	Ed. Alfred Hitchcock	Mayflower
Get Me to the Wake on Time	1973	Ed. Alfred Hitchcock	Mayflower
Strange Case of Dr Jekyll and Mr Hyde	1973	Robert Louis Stevenson	NEL
Murders I Fell in Love With	1973	Ed. Alfred Hitchcock	Mayflower
The Light That Never Was	1974	Lloyd Biggle, Jr	Morley
Stories They Wouldn't Let Me Do On TV 1	1974	Ed. Alfred Hitchcock	Pan
Stories They Wouldn't Let Me Do On TV 2	1974	Ed. Alfred Hitchcock	Pan
Seven Days in New Crete	1974	Robert Graves	Quartet
Stress Pattern	1974	Neal Barrett, Jr	DAW
The Mote in Time's Eye	1974	Gerard Klein	DAW

Title	Year	Author	Publisher
Entry to Elsewhen	1974	John Brunner	DAW
2018 A.D.	1974	Sam Lundwall	DAW
For Fear of Little Men	1974	John Blackburn	Sidgwick & Jackson
The End of the Dream	1974	Philip Wylie	Shire
Times Without Number	1974	John Brunner	Elmfield
Transit to Scorpio	1974	Alan Burt Akers	DAW
The Girl with a Symphony in Her Fingers	1975	Michael G. Coney	Elmfield
Wooden Centauri	1975	Paul Drennan	Elmfield
Warrior of Scorpio	1975	Alan Burt Akers	DAW
Suns of Scorpio	1975	Alan Burt Akers	DAW
The World's Best SF Short Stories No. 1	1975	Donald A. Wollheim	Elmfield
Patron of the Arts	1975	William Rotsler	Elmfield
The History of the Science Fiction Magazine 2	1975	Mike Ashley	NEL
The Moon Children	1975	Jack Williamson	Elmfield
Benedict's Planet	1975	James Corley	Elmfield
Pitman's Progress	1975	Douglas R. Mason	Elmfield
The Book of Philip José Farmer	1975	Philip José Farmer	Elmfield
Rax	1975	Michael G. Coney	DAW
Twilight of Briareus	1975	Richard Cowper	Quartet
Polymath	1975	John Brunner	DAW
Swordships of Scorpio	1975	Alan Burt Akers	DAW
Aldair in Albion	1976	Neal Barrett, Jr	DAW
A Whiff of Madness	1976	Ron Goulart	DAW
Prince of Scorpio	1976	Alan Burt Akers	DAW
A Darkness in My Soul	1976	Dean R. Koontz	DAW
Stories to be Read with the Lights On 1	1976	Ed. Alfred Hitchcock	Pan
The Panchronicon Plot	1976	Ron Goulart	DAW
Krozair of Kregen	1976	Alan Burt Akers	DAW
Stories to be Read with the Lights On 2	1977	Ed. Alfred Hitchcock	Pan
The Kraken Wakes	1977	John Wyndham	Longmans
Aldair, Master of Ships	1977	Neal Barrett, Jr	DAW
The Year's Best Fantasy Stories: 3	1977	Ed. Lin Carter	DAW
Mindbridge	1977	Joe Haldeman	Orbit
Secret Scorpio	1977	Alan Burt Akers	DAW
Calling Dr Patchwork	1977	Ron Goulart	DAW
Shock!	1977	Richard Matheson	Sphere
The Big Death	1977	Charles Eric Maine	Sphere
Shock II	1977	Richard Matheson	Sphere
Savage Scorpio	1978	Alan Burt Akers	DAW
Shock III	1978	Richard Matheson	Sphere
The Island Snatchers	1978	George H. Smith	DAW
Captive Scorpio	1978	Alan Burt Akers	DAW
The Wicked Cyborg	1978	Ron Goulart	DAW
Eloise	1978	E.C. Tubb	Arrow
Golden Scorpio	1978	Alan Burt Akers	DAW
Eye of the Zodiac	1978	E.C. Tubb	Arrow
Hello, Lemuria, Hello	1979	Ron Goulart	DAW
Morlock Night	1979	K.W. Jeter	DAW
Locusts	1979	Guy N. Smith	Hamlyn
Jack of Swords	1979	E.C. Tubb	Arrow
Journey to the Underground World	1979	Lin Carter	DAW
Haven of Darkness	1979	E.C. Tubb	Arrow
Spectrum of a Forgotten Sun	1979	E.C. Tubb	Arrow
Aldair, Across the Misty Sea	1979	Neal Barrett, Jr	DAW
Hail Hibbler	1980	Ron Goulart	DAW
The Year's Best Fantasy Stories: 6	1980	Ed. Lin Carter	DAW
Hurok of the Stone Age	1980	Lin Carter	DAW
The Robot in the Closet	1980	Ron Goulart	DAW
Darya of the Bronze Age	1981	Lin Carter	DAW
Lord Valentine's Castle	1981	Robert Silverberg	Pan
Upside Downside	1981	Ron Goulart	DAW
Eric of Zanthadon	1981	Lin Carter	DAW
Big Bang	1982	Ron Goulart	DAW
Aries Rising	1982	Arthur Herzog	Pan
Newfoundland	1982	John Christopher	Gollancz
Majipoor Chronicles	1983	Robert Silverberg	Pan
8th Armada Ghost Book	1983	Ed. Mary Danby	William Collins
11th Armada Ghost Book	1983	Ed. Mary Danby	William Collins
The Colour of Magic	1984	Terry Pratchett	Corgi
Valentine Pontifex	1984	Robert Silverberg	Pan
Wizards, Warriors and You			
(1) The Forest of Twisted Dreams	1984	R.L. Stine	Corgi
(2) The Siege of the Dragon Riders	1984	R.L. Stine	Corgi
(3) Who Kidnapped Princess Saralinda?	1984	R.L. Stine	Corgi
(4) Ghost Knights of Camelot	1984	R.L. Stine	Corgi
(5) The Haunted Castle of Ravencurse	1984	R.L. Stine	Corgi
(6) Revenge of the Falcon Knight	1984	R.L. Stine	Corgi

Tunnels and Trolls

Rule Book	1985	Ken St Andre	Corgi
Naked Doom	1985	Ken St Andre	Corgi
Deathtrap Equaliser	1985	Ken St Andre	Corgi
Beyond the Silvered Pane	1985	James and Steven Marciniak	Corgi
City of Terrors	1985	Michael A. Stackpole	Corgi
Sewers of Oblivion	1985	Michael A. Stackpole	Corgi
Sword for Hire	1985	James Wilson	Corgi
Blue Frog Tavern	1985	James Wilson	Corgi
Gamesmen of Karsar	1985	Roy Cram	Corgi
Mistywood	1985	Roy Cram	Corgi
Arena of Khazan	1985	Ken St Andre	Corgi
Amulet of Salkti	1985	David Steven Moskowitz	Corgi
Captive d'Yvoire	1985	James and Steven Marciniak	Corgi
Red Circle	1985	Michael A. Stackpole	Corgi
Caravan to Tiern	1985	Andrea Mills	Corgi
The Light Fantastic	1986	Terry Pratchett	Corgi
Equal Rites	1986	Terry Pratchett	Corgi

Duelmaster

No 1: Challenge of the Magi	1986	Mark Smith and	
Clash of the Magi	1986	Jamie Thomson	Collins
No 2: Blood Valley (1)	1986	Mark Smith and	
Blood Valley (2)	1986	Jamie Thomson	Collins
No 3: The Shattered Realm (1)	1986	Mark Smith and	
The Shattered Realm (2)	1987	Jamie Thomson	Collins
No 4: Arena of Death (1)	1987	Mark Smith and	
Arena of Death (2)	1987	Jamie Thomson	Collins
No 5: Hero King (1)	1987	Mark Smith and	
Hero King (2)	1987	Jamie Thomson	Collins
No 6: The Way of the Warrior (1)	1987	Mark Smith and	
The Way of the Warrior (2)	1987	Jamie Thomson	Collins
Nineteen Ninety Eight	1987	Richard Turner and William Osborne	Sphere
The Dark Side of the Sun	1987	Terry Pratchett	Corgi
Strata	1987	Terry Pratchett	Corgi
Mort	1987	Terry Pratchett	Gollancz
A Malady of Magicks	1988	Craig Shaw Gardner	Headline
The Brentford Trilogy	1988	Robert Rankin	Sphere
The Sprouts of Wrath	1988	Robert Rankin	Abacus
Sourcery	1988	Terry Pratchett	Gollancz
A Multitude of Monsters	1988	Craig Shaw Gardner	Headline
The Witches of Karres	1988	James H. Schmitz	Gollancz
Wyrd Sisters	1988	Terry Pratchett	Gollancz
A Night in the Netherhells	1988	Craig Shaw Gardner	Headline
A Difficulty with Dwarves	1988	Craig Shaw Gardner	Headline
Pyramids	1989	Terry Pratchett	Gollancz
An Excess of Enchantments	1989	Craig Shaw Gardner	Headline
Slaves of the Volcano God	1989	Craig Shaw Gardner	Headline
To Open the Sky	1989	Robert Silverberg	Sphere
Truckers	1989	Terry Pratchett	Doubleday
A Disagreement with Death	1989	Craig Shaw Gardner	Headline
Guards! Guards!	1989	Terry Pratchett	Gollancz
Here Be Demons	1989	Esther Friesner	Orbit
Bride of the Slime Monster	1989	Craig Shaw Gardner	Headline
Jason Cosmo	1989	Dan McGirt	Pan
Diggers	1989	Terry Pratchett	Doubleday
Revenge of the Fluffy Bunnies	1990	Craig Shaw Gardner	Headline
Demon Blues	1990	Esther Friesner	Orbit
Royal Chaos	1990	Dan McGirt	Pan
Wings	1990	Terry Pratchett	Doubleday
Eric	1990	Terry Pratchett and Josh Kirby	Gollancz
The Other Sinbad	1990	Craig Shaw Gardner	Headline
Moving Pictures	1990	Terry Pratchett	Gollancz
Quozl	1991	Alan Dean Foster	NEL
A Bad Day for Ali Baba	1991	Craig Shaw Gardner	Headline
Flying Dutch	1991	Tom Holt	Futura/Orbit
Expecting Someone Taller	1991	Tom Holt	Futura/|Orbit
Reaper Man	1991	Terry Pratchett	Gollancz
Who's Afraid of Beowulf?	1991	Tom Holt	Futura/Orbit
Eric (pb)	1991	Terry Pratchett	Gollancz
Witches Abroad	1991	Terry Pratchett	Gollancz
The Technicolor Time Machine	1991	Harry Harrison	Futura/Orbit
Hooray for Hellywood	1991	Esther Friesner	Futura/Orbit
Star Smashers of the Galaxy Rangers	1991	Harry Harrison	Futura/Orbit
Practical Demonkeeping	1991	Christopher Moore	Octopus
Scheherezade's Night Out	1991	Craig Shaw Gardner	Headline
Six Days	1991	Nick Page	Kingsway

Title	Year	Author	Publisher
Small Gods	1991	Terry Pratchett	Gollancz
The Carpet People	1992	Terry Pratchett	Corgi
Ye Gods!	1992	Tom Holt	Futura/Orbit
Overtime	1992	Tom Holt	Futura/Orbit
Lords and Ladies	1992	Terry Pratchett	Gollancz
Dirty Work	1992	Dan McGirt	Pan
Lords and Ladies (pb)	1993	Terry Pratchett	Corgi
Theatre of Cruelty	1993	Terry Pratchett	W. H. Smith Bookcase
Men at Arms	1993	Terry Pratchett	Gollancz
Strata	1993	Terry Pratchett	Doubleday
The Dark Side of the Sun	1993	Terry Pratchett	Doubleday
Raven Walking	1993	Craig Shaw Gardner	William Heinemann
Portraits of Terry Pratchett	1993		Weekend Guardian
Soul Music	1994	Terry Pratchett	Gollancz
Only You Can Save Mankind	1994	Terry Pratchett	Het Spectrum
The Discworld Companion	1994	Terry Pratchett and Stephen Briggs	Gollancz
Johnny and the Dead	1994	Terry Pratchett	Het Spectrum
The Witches Trilogy (picture from music CD)	1994	Terry Pratchett	Gollancz
Interesting Times	1994	Terry Pratchett	Gollancz
Dragon Waking	1994	Craig Shaw Gardner	William Heinemann
Interesting Times (pb)	1995	Terry Pratchett	Corgi
Maskerade	1995	Terry Pratchett	Gollancz
The Unseen University Challenge	1995	David Langford	Gollancz
The Wizards of Odd	1995	Ed. Peter Haining	Souvenir
Feet of Clay	1996	Terry Pratchett	Gollancz
The Wizards of Odd	1996	Ed. Peter Haining	Random House
Hogfather	1996	Terry Pratchett	Gollancz
Good Omens	1997	Terry Pratchett and Neil Gaiman	Heyne
The Flying Sorcerers	1997	Ed. Peter Haining	Souvenir
Jingo	1997	Terry Pratchett	Gollancz
Legends	1997	Robert Silverberg	Harper Collins
The Last Continent	1997	Terry Pratchett	Doubleday
Knights of Madness	1998	Ed. Peter Haining	Souvenir
Johnny and the Bomb	1998	Terry Pratchett	Wahlstrom Bokforlag
Carpe Jugulum	1998	Terry Pratchett	Doubleday
The Death Trilogy (picture from Eric)	1998	Terry Pratchett	Gollancz
The Flying Sorcerers	1998	Ed. Peter Haining	Little Brown
The Fifth Elephant	1999	Terry Pratchett	Doubleday

FILM POSTERS

Title	Year
Seven Cities to Atlantis/Warlords of the Deep	1978
Monty Python's Life of Brian	1979
Krull	1983
Beastmaster	1983
Starflight One	1983
Return of the Jedi	1983
Morons From Outer Space	1984

PORTFOLIO/BOOKS/COMPUTER GAMES/POSTERS, ETC.

Title	Year	Author	Publisher
Voyage of the Ayeguy (Limited Edition of 1,200 Prints) (Portfolio)	1981	Pacific Comics/Schanes & Schanes San Diego, California	
The Josh Kirby Poster Book	1990	Josh Kirby	Corgi
Eric	1990	Josh Kirby and Terry Pratchett	Gollancz
In the Garden of Unearthly Delights	1991	Josh Kirby and Nigel Suckling	Paper Tiger
The Josh Kirby Discworld Portfolio (Book)	1993	Josh Kirby	Paper Tiger
From the Discworld Album (Compact Disc)	1994	Dave Greenslade	Virgin
Discworld Computer Game	1994	Perfect Entertainment	Psygnosis
Rincewind and Luggage	1995	Poster	Isis
'Missing Presumed ...!?' – Computer Game II	1996	Perfect Entertainment	Psygnosis
Discworld Noir – Computer Game III	1999	Perfect Entertainment	GT Interactive
Discworld Calendar	1999		Ink Group
A Cosmic Cornucopia	1999	Josh Kirby and David Langford	Paper Tiger

Acknowledgements

David Langford is grateful for help, information and general support
provided during the writing of this text by Brian Ameringen, Alistair Durie,
Bernie Evans, Steve Holland, Patrick Janson-Smith, Stephen Jones, Hazel Langford,
Terry Pratchett, Christopher Priest, Andy Sawyer, Kenneth F. Slater, Colin Smythe,
Nigel Suckling, and above all Josh Kirby himself –
a copious and patient correspondent whose handwriting future
generations of archaeologists may one day decipher.

The Unseen University Challenge (Gollancz/Vista 1996), a quizbook compiled by David Langford.
Could this be the finest Discworld spinoff ever written? Kirby has amused himself by making
the contest wildly unequal: though Nanny Ogg has moments of competence, her hopeless team-mates
Detritus the thickwitted troll, Nobby of the Watch and Rincewind have no chance against high-flyers
Death, Angua, Carrot and Granny Weatherwax.